Words
No Bars Can Hold

Advance Praise

"The equitable distribution of powerful literacy education is among the most serious human rights issues of our time. Far beyond mere reading and writing, Appleman reminds us that a true learning is an act of Freedom. In this perspective, she joins a long tradition of activists, revolutionaries, gurus, newly emancipated slaves, artists, and griots who have spoken of the liberatory power of the Word. Appleman is the conscience of the field when it comes to emancipatory education for the incarcerated and her newest work offers a pedagogical and moral challenge to educators and others interested in social justice and a truly human dialogue. In *Words No Bars Can Hold*, Appleman introduces us to the pedagogical theories and the stories of real people who want what we all want, to live lives of decency and dignity and to be heard and listened to. An educator cannot read this book without being challenged to see all people differently, to recognize his or her complicity in the prison industrial complex, and to insist on literacy instruction rooted in agency, voice, power, and love."

—Ernest Morrell, Ph.D., Coyle Professor in Literacy Education, Professor, English and Africana Studies, Director, Center for Literacy Education, University of Notre Dame

"Deborah Appleman brings a wealth of experience to this stirring and thought-provoking account of teaching in prison. Reading it, we learn so much about the power of writing, about teaching, about what education makes possible, and about the urgent human capacity to define who we are."

—Mike Rose, author of *Back to School: Why Everyone Deserves a Second Chance at Education*

"In *Words No Bars Can Hold*, Deborah Appleman culminates years of teaching and writing in a book that spans spaces rarely brought together: the public school, the liberal arts college, and the community of prison authors. The result is an eloquent meditation on how the art of narrative defines what it is we mean by education itself, and its centrality to what Appleman calls the potential for 'self-rehabilitation.' An extended celebration of critical pedagogies, it persuades its readers by devoting many of its pages to extended selections from the writings of accomplished authors who have been, or still are, incarcerated."

—Daniel Karpowitz, author of *College in Prison: Reading in an Age of Mass Incarceration*

"*Words No Bars Can Hold* sharpens our analysis and does the necessary work to break our hearts. Deborah Appleman's evocative writing—a powerful form of witnessing to the lives and literacies of people who struggle to survive life in a cage—propels readers to recognize that we must build the world we need and imagine and make other pathways to accountability, to healing, and to justice that do not involve death by incarceration. Our lives and communities depend on it. Written with a fluid and accessible voice, this essential text invites a wide range of readers to view radical literacy work as a key tool to strengthen national movements to end our prison nation."

—**Erica R. Meiners, Ph.D., Bernard J. Brommel Distinguished Research Professor, Northeastern Illinois University**

"Do the liberal arts actually liberate? Deborah Appleman proves they can. Her work with incarcerated students demonstrates the power of reading, critical thinking, and creative writing to change lives from the inside out. *Words No Bars Can Hold* is a guidebook both for those looking to improve education within correctional institutions as well as for those of us working to keep students far away from the school-to-prison pipeline. An important book."

—**Carol Jago, high school English teacher, past president of the National Council of Teachers of English, author of *The Book in Question: Why and How Reading Is in Crisis***

"From the prelude to the conclusion, Appleman's book is dripping with kernels of humanity. Her life and commitment to the role of education for those behind bars signal what it means to be a disciple of good. I anticipate this will become a seminal text for those who want to educate men in one of our nation's darkest spaces."

—**Alfred W. Tatum, Ph.D., Dean, UIC College of Education**

Words
No Bars Can Hold

Literacy Learning in Prison

DEBORAH APPLEMAN

W. W. NORTON & COMPANY
Independent Publishers Since 1923
New York • London

"The Last Visit From the Girl in the Willow Tree" reprinted by permission of PEN America

PEN America stands at the intersection of literature and human rights to protect free expression in the United States and worldwide. The organization champions the freedom to write, recognizing the power of the word to transform the world. Join, follow, and donate at pen.org.

For information about permission to reproduce selections from this book, write to Permissions, W. W. Norton & Company, Inc., 500 Fifth Avenue, New York, NY 10110

For information about special discounts for bulk purchases, please contact W. W. NortonSpecial Sales at specialsales@wwnorton.com or 800-233-4830

Manufacturing by Lake Book Manufacturing, Inc.
Book design by Vicki Fischman
Production manager: Katelyn MacKenzie

Library of Congress Cataloging-in-Publication Data

Names: Appleman, Deborah, author.
Title: Words no bars can hold : literacy learning in prison / Deborah Appleman.
Description: First edition. | New York : W.W. Norton & Company, [2019] |
    Includes bibliographical references and index.
Identifiers: LCCN 2018050856 | ISBN 9780393713671 (hardcover)
Subjects: LCSH: Prisoners—Education—United States. | Criminals—
    Rehabilitation—United States. | Literacy programs—UnitedStates. |
    Education and crime—United States.
Classification: LCC HV8883.3.U5 A66 2019 | DDC 365/.6660973—dc23
LC record available at https://lccn.loc.gov/2018050856

W. W. Norton & Company, Inc., 500 Fifth Avenue, New York, N.Y. 10110
www.wwnorton.com

W. W. Norton & Company Ltd., 15 Carlisle Street, London W1D 3BS

1 2 3 4 5 6 7 8 9 0

Dedicated to the memory of two extraordinary mothers
FAYE APPLEMAN WEIL
PAMELA J. CALIGUIRI

Also by Deborah Appleman

Adolescent Literacies: A Handbook of Practice-Based Research
Editor, with Kathleen A. Hinchman

Teaching Literature to Adolescents, Third Edition
with Richard Beach, Bob Fecho, and Rob Simon

*Critical Encounters in Secondary English: Teaching
Literary Theory to Adolescents, Third Edition*

*UnCommon Core: What the Authors of the Standards Got
Wrong About Instruction—and How You Can Get it Right*
with Michael W. Smith and Jeffrey D. Wilhelm

*Reading Better, Reading Smarter: Designing
Literature Lessons for Adolescents*
with Michael F. Graves

*Adolescent Literacy and the Teaching of Reading:
Lessons for Teachers of Literature*

*From the Inside Out: Letters to Young Men and
Other Writings, Poetry and Prose from Prison*
Editor

*Reading for Themselves: How to Transform Adolescents
into Lifelong Readers Through Out-of-Class Book Clubs*

Braided Lives: An Anthology of Multicultural American Writing
Co-chair, editorial board

Everybody is better than the worst they've ever done.
—*Willie Earl Lloyd Jr.*
convicted of murder at 18, freed after 23 years in prison

Education is freedom.
—*Paulo Freire*

CONTENTS

FOREWORD   **xiii**

ACKNOWLEDGMENTS   **xvii**

PRELUDE
Education: Life or Death   xix

CHAPTER ONE
A Tough Sell: Education and Incarceration   1
   Blog Entry: Fist Bump Through the Bars   9

CHAPTER TWO
The Geography of Incarceration: The Glass Bubble
in the Big House   11
   *Blog Entry: "How to Do a Full Body Workout
in Your Cell"; Or, Lesson Planning in Prison*   17

CHAPTER THREE
Of Freire and Frost: Reading the World Behind Bars   19
   Blog Entry: Tony and the Blue Book   28

CHAPTER FOUR
"No Hugs for Thugs": Surveillance and Control   31
   Blog Entry: Saying Goodbye to Grandma in Chains   40

CHAPTER FIVE
"I Will Write Myself Out of Prison": Rewriting the Self   41
   Blog Entry: Knowledge Is Truly Food For Our Souls   56

CHAPTER SIX

Writing in the Dark: Profiles of Incarcerated Learners   58

    Blog Entry: Sticks and Stones   94

CHAPTER SEVEN

"What If I Had Started to Write in High School?":
Interrupting the School-to-Prison Pipeline   98

    Blog Entry: School-to-Prison Pipeline   116

CHAPTER EIGHT

"Songs from the Genius Child": Words No Bars Can Hold   118

    Blog Entry: Stay Free   139

EPILOGUE

Thoughts Beyond the Bars: The Dark and the Light   141

REFERENCES   147

SELECTIONS OF WRITING BY INCARCERATED WRITERS   153

INDEX   155

I could mire the reader in statistics, data, and the graphs and charts and maps that prove education for prisoners works: but take my word for it, I am evidence of that. Once you start to read this book, *Words No Bars Can Hold*, you realize there's something larger at work here than just another testimony of someone's experience teaching creative writing (and more) in prison. Deborah Appleman leads us into the prison world and humanizes the prisoners, connects with them, unveils their sorrows and joys, works the environment until we often seem we're right beside her and can hear the breathing of the quiet cells, see the dreams of the men as they sleep, accompany them in their hopes and sorrows, on their individual journeys to reclaim their humanity.

It's much more, of course, and it works to bring full force the problems, the solutions, the alternating dynamics that have so often stymied the concerned citizen in the past. Deborah manages to balance out the pros and cons with rational insights that cannot be conveyed except through years of sacrifice and service. Her vocation and mission is not to righteously pose herself on a soapbox and rage about the wrongs and accuse—no: but to take us on a genuine search that leads to trial and error until she understands what unfolds as true growth, individual awareness and a reckoning that leads to change. That's what this book does, it carries us through the various levels, in prose that is clear and well thought out; showing how creative writing workshops work to salvage the human being's last remnants of self-esteem and allow the prisoner to give freedom another shot—and thus, not return to prison.

We arrive with her, but not in all the do-gooder blather of holier-than-thou Samaritan piety; here, Deborah gets dirty, crawls in the trenches, exhausts her patience, sometimes belabors to believe. And in the end her perseverance and faith prove what no statistics and numbers can reflect: that through bulldogged commitment to a deep belief, seeing it through, one realizes that yes, indeed, creative writing does work to help prisoners find themselves, to improve their chances at making it on the outside. It encourages them to continue in their education, to believe again in themselves, to trust, to try to love and live again.

There will always be the grim naysayers, the extreme conservatives that just see punishment as an end-all to every problem. Nothing, not all the proof in the world, will serve to convince them otherwise. There are some, especially in this Age of Cynicism, that will never be moved by truth.

But if you're open to creative positive change, then read *Words No Bars Can Hold*. This wonderful book proposes that education not only enhances the chances a prisoner will never come back to prison; education ensures, more than any other factor can, that after leaving prison that person's life will be a productive contribution to society.

Some progressive colleges like Bard do amazing work with educating prisoners and should be lauded and funded and serve as a model for other colleges. It's good for the students engaged in these programs, too; it helps the free and the imprisoned. What more could you ask for in pursuit of a more peaceful and judicial society.

Providing a liberal arts education for prisoners is like breaking the seal of silence and opening a whole host of opportunities for men and women who have never had them—an effective way to usher in success, leave behind failure. There are tons of books and studies that prove it works, but rare is the one that takes us on such a profound journey: from the warden to guards to the prisoners and beyond, right down to the children of incarcerated men and women who say it works to improve their lives and relationships with their families and friends.

Rather than neglect the problem of crime and pipeline-from-school-to-prison tragedy, Deborah Appleman launches into the opportunity to educate and help these prisoners grow and learn: she invites them to participate in the grand experiment of writing and reading, and use literacy as a tool to become productive citizens. The alternative would be to decide to close themselves in their rooms and pout; but she stands there, with the door open, beckoning them to engage with her--and they do. It's co-liberation.

Her book seems to whisper on every page, "...we must go ahead with our dreams and we will and do." Basic literacy obstacles are confronted, unscalable heights of emotional traumas challenged, until these students achieve the dream to read and write and restore and reclaim their humanity.

She nails it in this book: how the classroom becomes a refuge of trust among the writers and poets in her writing class. How another level of humanity is reached through literature and writing. She gives us overviews of her teaching experience, personalizes the narrative with a life devoted to those incarcerated, of someone with a daunting and passionate commitment to prison reform through education.

Deborah does more than advocate for education; she illustrates for readers the amazing transformation the participant undergoes when determined to teach himself to read and write. She offers an extraordinary look at how humanity unfolds as fear is released, as trust is enhanced. We see each individual reaching out of his hostile environment to touch the world beyond with gentler, more peaceful hands and mind.

She investigates ways to stop the destruction that happens when the pipeline from schools to prisons is carrying away our kids to one-way dead-ends. The poems and writings are all a testament to the depth and passion and earnestness with which these participants embraced the education that allowed them to express their humanity.

The blog posts between chapters take us on a journey from the inside of the author's heart and mind to the world that she enters every day, going from one place that is free into another place made of concrete and steel and sustained by fear and nightmares. And in part it's the contrast she so aptly poses between these places—the college and the prison classroom—that makes this book so valuable. Appleman is a true warrior fighting the good fight. The valiant fight that makes a life worth living, gives it purpose and during hard times protects it with the fabric of grace. Grace that can only arrive through great sacrifice and joy in one's work.

I can't overstate how you need to read this book, carry it with you, pass it off to friends, take it to class, share it at dinner tables, open it at a coffee shop, quote from it—you'll be sharing in work that is profoundly important today. Prison education is the climate change nucleus of our social tragedy, and it can lead us toward the light. Unerringly, in ways that only someone who given her life to writing programs in prison can, she invites us to come along, and gives in a few hours of reading what has taken her a lifetime to gather and offer us: an immeasurable gift of awareness and knowledge, deeply needed today.

Jimmy Santiago Baca

ACKNOWLEDGMENTS

Thank you to Mike Rose. Through your wisdom, you taught me how to place humanity at the center of education. Through your prose, you taught me how to write about it.

The writing of this book was made possible by a generous Faculty Development Grant from Carleton College. The gift of time is priceless.

I owe a special thank-you to my dear colleagues Nancy Cho and Melinda Russell for their friendship and for the support and camaraderie I found in our writing group.

Thanks to my colleague Jeffrey Snyder, who is as generous and kind as he is smart.

Thank you to my partners in this work who help make it sustainable through their own work and their friendship: Peter Williamson, Erick Gordon, and Jennifer Bowen Hicks.

Thanks to Jimmy Santiago Baca for his endless inspiration to writers and teachers everywhere, both inside and out.

Special thanks go to Lillie Schneyer for her expert editing and thoughtful reading.

Thanks to Mandy Duong for her assistance.

Thank you to Annie Larson for her patience with me in all things and for her help with the manuscript preparation.

Thanks to John Schmit, who knows both my best and my worst selves and who helped keep the worst one at bay during the writing of this book.

A very special thank-you goes to Carol Chambers Collins, my first and best editor. Her vision and support helped make this book possible.

Finally, I thank my incarcerated students. Through your resilience, strength, and insight, you have taught me more than I will ever teach you. Nothing can quench your thirst for learning. No bars can hold your words.

Education: Life or Death

H E DROVE TO OUR MEETING. It seems mundane, a daily detail we take for granted, but for a formerly incarcerated person, it was a significant passage. The keys to the battered black Honda lay proudly on the restaurant table, an announcement of his complete liberation.

"Willie gave me this car." Willie served time with Eli in prison and has been out long enough to have upgraded his beater.

As Eli sat across from me, I noticed all the tokens of freedom he seemed to have amassed in such a short time: well-polished dress shoes, a smartphone, an iPad, a fashion-forward watch, even a business card. I couldn't help but flash back to the baby-faced man in prison grays who sat in the very front of the first class I ever taught in a prison. It was an Introduction to Literature class, replete with a Norton anthology and literary criticism cards. Eli sat in front, next to Willie, devouring each literary text and its analysis. It was in that class that I first realized the power of teaching and learning behind bars for the incarcerated students and for the teacher. It was Eli, then serving a life sentence with seemingly no out date, who pushed me to consider the pure, nonpragmatic, nonvocational value of learning for learning's sake.

What is the value of liberal education? he once asked me.

To liberate, I replied automatically and unthinkingly, blushing at the insensitivity of the response to someone who had spent nearly twenty years behind bars and had a lifetime of incarceration stretching in front of him.

Yes, he said, I knew you would say that. This learning will make us free.

Back at the restaurant, his manners were almost exaggeratingly proper, eating fish and chips with a knife and fork, making up for all those hurriedly and unceremoniously ingested prison meals. We talked about the different building blocks that comprised his slowly reconstructed life: good: work, plenty of successful networking, mastery of social media, and ambitious plans for the future; not so good: a precarious marriage to someone who had befriended him in prison.

When we began talking about the possibility of him visiting a school in the urban center of the city we now share, to work with black adolescent males, his eyes lit up.

That's what it's all about: education. How can I let them see what I learned without them having to go to prison to learn it? My life changed when I started learning; it shifted my paradigm. *Educare*: to bring out, to bring forth. That's what you taught me and it made all the difference. I realized that there was something of value inside me, living beside the regret, the recriminations, the broken promises.

I have to learn to do it, to do for them what you and others have done for me.

We can work both ends of the pipeline—right? Move backward so that the guys who are still inside can see what education can do for them. It ain't over, maybe they can all get out someday. And then for those young brothers, let's try to capture them together—with learning. Maybe they don't need to do time to learn my hard lessons. But we gotta do it—it's a matter of life and death.

This was Eli, the autodidact—given a life sentence at fifteen, barely able to read and write. He became his own teacher and his own lawyer and eventually was able to get his sentenced overturned.

I watched my student turning into a teacher, the incarcerated becoming free, and I began to realize that I will never do anything more important than be a teacher to men like Eli.

It isn't what we teach that matters; it's who we teach that does.

Words
No Bars Can Hold

CHAPTER ONE

A Tough Sell

EDUCATION AND INCARCERATION

I T'S A TOUGH SELL, higher education for the incarcerated. Despite the euphemistic use of the term "correction," most penal institutions are in the business of punishment. It seems primal, almost biblical, this human inclination to want to punish. We extend that inclination into wanting to make sure that nothing good happens to people whom we deem to be bad. If education is good, then bad people shouldn't get it.

Even tougher to sell than the general notion of education is the idea of liberal arts education for the incarcerated. Vocational training—welding, carpentry, computer programming, etc.—makes sense to provide future job opportunities for those who will eventually be released. But general liberal education, with no real-world value, especially for those serving life sentences? It's a tough sell, indeed. But it's what I am selling.

This book focuses on the potential role of liberal arts education for the incarcerated and on the ways in which postsecondary education in general and creative writing opportunities in particular can help reframe the personal narratives of the incarcerated, especially for those serving life sentences. It will also consider the school-to-prison pipeline or nexus from the sobering perspective of the end of the pipeline, since most of the students with whom I have worked are serving life sentences in a state that no longer offers parole.

In the twenty-first century, the United States incarcerates more of its citizens than any other country. On any given day, more than one in every 100 adults are in jail or prison (Pew, 2009). Although there were an estimated 6,899,000 people (2.8% of American adults) within adult correction systems in 2013, the incarcerated remain nearly invisible to most of society. As Alexander (2010) argues, incarceration has become the new caste system in the United States.

Despite incontrovertible evidence of the powerful effects of education on recidivism, education programs in prison have diminished or disappeared as a result of restrictions on funding such as Pell grants and the chilling effects of tough-on-crime legislation. Across the country, funding has dried up for prison programs, especially those located in high- or maximum-security prisons. As Martin (2009) explains:

> The tough-on-crime era of the 1970s and after ushered in a host of measures that supported the framework of a harsher, more punitive approach to prisoners. . . . Mandatory minimum sentencing, three-strikes-and-you're out sentencing laws, juveniles being tried as adults—all of these were part of the trend. Amid all this, the defunding of education programs for prisoners was a less noticed but related change.

Offerings in prison have dwindled to just a handful of largely technical courses. Libraries have become sparse and outdated; technology is used only sparingly and is compromised by constant surveillance and worries of security breaches. Many potential students are ineligible for the classes they are so eager to take because of their status as violent offenders. In other words, those who are most likely to benefit from the positive outcomes of postsecondary education are prevented from taking part in it. In "Unlocking Potential: Results of a National Survey of Postsecondary Education in State Prisons," a report from the Institute for Higher Education Policy, the authors found that

> [a]lthough research has shown a link between educating prisoners and reduced rates of recidivism, many inmates have struggled to pay for college since President Bill Clinton barred inmates from receiving Pell Grants in 1994. Some private colleges have joined with nearby

prisons to offer free, for-credit courses to inmates, but those individual partnerships, while often successful in reducing recidivism on a small scale, don't represent the educational opportunities available to most inmates. (Sieben, 2011)

To be sure, there are a few notable exceptions to this dire portrait of prison education programs. Both Bard College and Grinnell College offer prison programs that present "liberal arts behind bars." Bard College has an extensive program that works with five New York prisons.

While these two programs have clearly animated the potential of offering liberal arts to the incarcerated, they exist as isolated beacons of light in an otherwise dark landscape of missed opportunities. So what can liberal arts education do for the incarcerated? Why should this particular kind of education, often associated with elite colleges and students of privilege, be offered to the incarcerated? I intend to answer these questions in my book.

Harris (1991) describes "a liberal arts education" as one that teaches individuals how to think, how to learn, how to make sense of the world around them, how to understand the relationship between old knowledge and new knowledge, and how to generate creativity. He writes:

> The diverse body of knowledge you will gain from a liberal arts education, together with the tools of examination and analysis that you will learn to use, will enable you to develop your own opinions, attitudes, values, and beliefs, based not upon the authority of parents, peers, or professors, and not upon ignorance, whim, or prejudice, but upon your own worthy apprehension, examination, and evaluation of argument and evidence. . . . A thorough knowledge of a wide range of events, philosophies, procedures, and possibilities makes the phenomena of life appear coherent and understandable. No longer will unexpected or strange things be merely dazzling or confusing. (2010)

Brown University (2013) also delineates some important results of liberal arts education, including enhancing communication skills such as writing and speaking, understanding differences among cultures, evaluating human behavior, embracing diversity, learning what it means to study the past, collaborating fully, experiencing scientific inquiry, developing a facility with symbolic languages, expanding reading skills, enhancing aesthetic sensibility, and applying what one has learned. These are broad intellectual goals, to be sure, but goals that are relevant for the incarcerated as well. As Nixon writes, "Education should also be considered on its own merit. Put simply: education is not just a means to myriad positive ends, but an end unto itself. Education—on its own—is worth pursuing, worth having and worth supporting" (Nixon, 2012).

Although it may seem counterintuitive, liberal arts education is particularly well suited to the incarcerated, especially those who are serving very long sentences. The lack of specific vocational focus, sometimes viewed as a shortcoming for those on the outside, is actually advantageous for those who are drawn to experiences whose value is not tied to vocational training. For many of the incarcerated, these programs provide a second chance to avail themselves of the value of education, a value that they might not previously have experienced. Many prisoners are likely to have poor self-confidence and negative attitudes about education because they viewed their early experiences as being negative (Paul, 1991).

While many of the incarcerated with whom I have worked seem to have had ambivalent feelings about education on the outside, it becomes a cherished experience for most on the inside. At a panel featuring Grinnell's Liberal Arts in Prison Program (February 3, 2013), a recently released former student spoke enthusiastically about what the liberal arts had done for him: "Liberal arts changed me to the core. The liberal arts teach you how to think. Vocational education may teach you how to perform a job, but liberal arts education teaches you about yourself." Another member of the panel said, "The outside world falls away when you are institutionalized. The world outside of prison becomes an abstract idea. Liberal arts education makes that world come back to you. As you grapple with ideas, you are grappling with the world."

One important element of liberal arts education is the ability to express one's ideas and learning through writing, both expository and creative. While literacy researchers in the fields of composition, creative writing, reading and literature, and adult education have rightfully expanded their focus to include many kinds of diverse learners, little attention has historically been paid to the literacy learning of the incarcerated (Greenberg, Dunleavy, and Kutner, 2007).

While the courses that I have taught have included both kinds of writing, my focus has been more weighted to creative writing. Recently, there has been a renewal of interest in how the teaching of creative writing might provide important opportunities for the incarcerated (Appleman, 2013). Rogers (2008) focuses on the pedagogical considerations relevant to teaching creative writing to the incarcerated. *PMLA* published a suite of articles on in-prison education, including studies about the impact of literature on the lives of the incarcerated (Waxler, 2008), the literary accomplishments of the incarcerated (Franklin, 2008), productions of Shakespeare by and for offenders at correctional facilities in Wisconsin and Massachusetts (Shailor, 2008; Trounstine, 2008), and the appropriateness of higher education within prison settings (Lewen, 2008). Still, opportunities for creative writing in prison, especially prisoner-sponsored programs, are rare (Appleman, 2013). More rarely still have prison efforts been considered in the context of liberal arts education as a whole (Bard Prison Collective, 2013).

In particular, the pedagogy of creative writing, with its emphasis on identity construction and narration, seems to provide an impetus for innovation, as the incarcerated writers reshaped their personal narratives and decided to claim personal power through their writing to the degree that they were able to do so. They formed a collective to publish a book (*From the Inside Out: Letters to Young Men and Other Writings*, 2009), held group sessions for aspiring writers, secured more creative writing opportunities for fellow prisoners, and created a restorative justice program that donated proceeds from their book to causes of healing and reparation.

According to correctional officials, the writers who participated in the education program were less likely to engage in behavior warranting reprimand in the cellblocks, and they improved their attendance at other prison programs as well. Several joined the staff of the prison newspaper, *The Prison Mirror*, which happens to be the oldest-running prison newspaper in the United States.

This offers some evidence that the pedagogy of creative writing, with its emphasis on identity construction and narration, seems to provide opportunities for self-reflection as well as powerful clues to where the life courses of these incarcerated students might have been altered. Through narrative and oral history, prisoners explore and interrogate their own sense of identity. Through successful literacy learning experiences, incarcerated learners are able to readjust their sense of themselves as writers and readers with literate lives. Finally, recent research reveals that the more education a prisoner has when he is released, the less likely he or she is to reoffend (Bard College, n.d.).

On the other hand, there were several writers who, despite their efforts in the classes, continued to have disciplinary and personal issues within the prison. Their experiences remind us to resist the overly romantic notion that literacy programs can become a panacea for the incarcerated. Words are powerful but not magical, and these writers and their continued struggle remind us of the limits of these efforts. Liberal education does not allow the incarcerated, or their teachers for that matter, to transcend the persistent social, educational, and economic problems (Trounstine, 2008). Without undercutting the power of those literacy narratives that are produced and celebrated, the book calls for a more realistic frame through which to view literacy education in prison (Davis, 2011).

Thus far, my work offers some evidence that, through successful literacy learning experiences, most incarcerated learners readjust their stance within the context of the prison, begin to seek advanced degrees (Yagelski, 2000), and sometimes even initiate contact with victims or their victims' families through the Restorative Justice Program. This program is designed to help the incarcerated come to terms with their crimes by making them accountable to their victims in a variety of ways. They write apology letters that are stored until the victim's family requests them. Occasionally, as was the case for two of my students, they actually meet face to face with the victim's family. In some ways these incarcerated students attempt to write themselves back into a society that has erased their lived histories. The student work presented in this book will demonstrate the transformative power of education to promote self-efficacy and literacy in even the most dehumanizing of circumstances.

Finally, as educators become aware that youth caught up in school disciplinary webs are more likely to be retained in grades, pushed out of school, commit a crime, and/or end up incarcerated as adults, this book seeks to offer some insight from the narratives of those who were caught in the school-to-prison pipeline.

The rest of the book is organized in the following way. Each chapter is followed by an excerpt from a blog I kept while teaching full-time at the prison during a sabbatical. The entries are not presented in chronological order, but rather by the resonance they have to the chapters they follow.

CHAPTER 2: The Geography of Incarceration: The Glass Bubble in the Big House

This chapter describes the context of the education program at the prison where I teach. It contrasts the "Shawshank" grittiness of the rest of the prison with the physical and psychological oasis that the classroom provides.

CHAPTER 3: Of Freire and Frost: Reading the World Behind Bars

In this chapter, I describe the teaching and learning dynamic of the classes I taught as well as the tutoring program, where educated prisoners tutor others for basic literacy and GED preparation.

CHAPTER 4: "No Hugs for Thugs": Surveillance and Control

The limits and controls imposed by the Department of Corrections (DOC) hold teachers hostage as well as students. This chapter explores the constraints on teaching and learning and provides an analysis of why such limits exist.

CHAPTER 5: "I Will Write Myself Out of Prison": Rewriting the Self

This chapter focuses on the ways in which the incarcerated students' educational experiences help them reframe their sense of self and their personal narratives. In several cases, student writing also had an impact on corrections officials and caused changes in students' sentences and even prison transfers from maximum to minimum security facilities.

CHAPTER 6: Writing in the Dark: Profiles of Incarcerated Learners

Four very different prisoners—diverse in age, ethnicity, length of time incarcerated, previous education, and length of sentence—will be profiled, focusing on how education is situated within their lives. Excerpts from their own work, ranging from poetry to memoir and academic writing, is integrated into the chapter.

CHAPTER 7: "What If I Had Started to Write in High School?": Interrupting the School-to-Prison Pipeline

This chapter explores the relationship between current socioeconomic and educational realities and the prison population. Using examples of two programs from city high schools, where I have also worked regularly, the chapter will explore ways in which secondary schools might work to interrupt the school-to-prison pipeline.

CHAPTER 8: "Songs from the Genius Child": Words No Bars Can Hold

This chapter offers a sampling of the poetry and prose written by the incarcerated students I have taught. Using different genres, topics, and perspectives, the writing helps present a concluding argument about the role liberal arts education can and should play in the lives of America's incarcerated population.

Fist Bump Through the Bars

My well-equipped prison classroom sometimes leads me to overlook the conditions of incarceration that are a reality of my students' lives. A serendipitous visit to a cellblock changed all that. I had arranged to have writing conferences for each of my students to return their unbelievably cool writing portfolios. I met with each student for half an hour in the classroom and offered them suggestions for their growth as writers. It's the stuff of Writing Pedagogy 101, except when it takes place in a prison.

On this particular day, I'm scheduled to meet with Twin. I know him well because he has taken every class I've taught in the prison. He looks a bit like a miniature Malcolm X—slight in stature, with thick black glasses. He's a true autodidact, too. He's been incarcerated since he was fifteen (he's over thirty now) and has taught himself almost everything he knows, and he knows a lot.

I find out that Twin is in lockdown because of an incident with a staff member. He can't come out to meet me. I feel frustrated and deeply disappointed. This is my last chance to see him and to give him back his work. And then, an extraordinary thing happens. The prison staff grants me permission to see Twin in his cell. I'd been teaching in the prison for two years, knowing full well that at this high-security prison, I was teaching violent offenders who spent most of their time locked up. However, the classroom in which we met was quite regular in appearance and served to normalize our interactions. I never really saw the students locked up or behaving in any way that wasn't predictable within the normal classroom context. So I let myself forget about where we were, and I just taught them. It was what I thought I should do. Somehow, I had not faced the harsh reality of their incarceration. Until now. Seeing Twin in his cell reminded me of what I was really dealing with.

I walked gingerly down through the cellblock and found Twin's cell. There was nothing in it except a photo of a fellow cellmate who had committed suicide a few months before. The cell was 6 by 9, lit only by a bare bulb. In typical Twin fashion, he was writing and a thick thesaurus and dictionary lay on his bare steel cot.

He quickly jumped up, brushed himself off, and looked at me with a mixture of delight and embarrassment. Was I wrong to let him be seen by me this way? Did this moment of seeing him behind bars erase the countless hours I saw him think and write and read like a free man?

When the conference was over we did a fist bump through the bars, and I turned away quickly so he couldn't see my tears.

For better or worse, the last thing I'll remember is seeing Twin in his cold bare cell, a mere suggestion of the man I came to know in our oasis of teaching and learning.

CHAPTER TWO

The Geography of Incarceration

THE GLASS BUBBLE IN THE BIG HOUSE

PRISONS ARE MISLEADING PLACES. They house departments of "correction," but, despite the best intentions of some very good people who work there, they all too often function as departments of punishment. Even the architecture is designed to mask the grim reality of life behind bars. Take the foyer of this prison, for instance. The name of the facility is engraved above the entryway in big fancy letters on a brass plaque. The walls are pink marble, trimmed in a warm rich wood, maybe walnut. There are massive wood doors with brass handles leading into byzantine halls of offices for the warden and associate wardens. There is no sign of the din within, of the five tiers of cells, of the peeling painted metal, of the dashed dreams and hopelessness that lie behind the double-locked doors.

First built in 1910, this prison was designed in the "telephone pole" layout, with a large main hallway that connects the units or cellblocks. Each of those units is five tiers tall, with metal bars throughout. Individual cells are 6 feet by 9 feet. Due to the small size and safety/security concerns, prisoners are permitted to keep only two small footlockers of personal belongings. I've overheard men agonizing over which books to shed as they acquire new ones and simply don't have room to store them all. Each housing section has what's called the flag, named so because it was originally made of flagstone. The flag is the epicenter of social activity, where card games like Texas Hold 'Em are played, where phone calls, preciously expensive, are made and received, and where, the warden tells me, animated intellectual discussions occur when the students are taking classes. Plato on the flag. Beautiful.

At one end of the foyer, amiable uniformed guards chat easily behind a glass partition. I hand them my license, strip off all jewelry and shoes and barrettes, anything with metal. I hope I remembered to wear my prison bra, the one without the underwire. I walk through a metal detector, so discriminating that it puts all airport security to shame. Every time I go through this ritual, I feel humiliated by it. Even though I am innocent, I feel guilty, powerless, and stripped of the talismans of my identity, my government-issued photo ID.

This ritual establishes and reinforces some important dynamics of working in prisons: they are in control; I am not. I am subject to their clearly articulated procedures. I must cooperate or lose the privilege of entering. My status as a college professor or even as a free person doesn't matter in here. The Panopticon, the relentless surveillance in the service of safety and control, is at work.

My class materials—books, handouts, student papers—are in a specially ordered see-through plastic book bag. The guard carefully thumbs through each book to make sure I am not smuggling any contraband. My right hand is stamped with invisible ink, which will be scanned with a fluorescent flashlight on my way out to make sure it is I who returns and not a cross-dressing imposter in a red wig, carrying out an improbable escape. "It happens," a guard explains. "You'd be surprised." Yes, I think to myself, I would be.

I walk slowly through a long hallway, my high heels clicking incongruously on the hard floor. I always dress up, making use of the same signal of sartorial respect that I've always shown my students, wherever they are. What we are doing together, this learning, is worth dressing up for. You are worth dressing up for. The rules for dress for volunteers are very specific, anyway: no leggings, sleeveless shirts, scarves, opentoed shoes, skirts, shorts, or knee-high boots.

I walk by a stand of guards. It might be my imagination, but I feel like they are amused by me, perhaps even contemptuous of the naivete of a "do-gooder" who really doesn't know what these men are like most of the time, that her beloved students are monsters who live in cages sixteen out of twenty-four hours.

Usually I make the long walk to the classroom alone, but sometimes there is "movement" between the mess hall and the blocks or between the walled-in exercise pen back into the prison. Then, dozens of men of all ages and sizes stream by. A few recognize me and nod slightly, almost imperceptibly. Others stare curiously.

There is a wing of the prison, separated from the rest of the building by a long hallway and a separate guard station, that is the education wing. With glass walls and gleaming desks and functional, if not up-to-date computer stations, the education wing stands in stark contrast to other parts of the prison, in both function and appearance. There is a library, filled with books and journals, definitely not the most current version of *The Atlantic*, or even *Time* or *Newsweek*, but a decent collection nonetheless. There has been a parade of librarians from an incredibly cheerful and helpful woman named Debbie who comported herself as if she was serving avid readers in a serene suburb, to her successor, whose deer-in-the-headlights look foreshowed her short stay and hasty departure. "She's scared of us," one of my students confided.

At the end of the walkway, I climb a few stairs; the classroom area is elevated—fitting, I think, the prison version of the ivory tower. There are two more guards behind glass; they nod in recognition and give me a "screecher," a plastic circle with a noisemaker inside. Just in case, they offer as an explanation. I hide it so the men don't think I am afraid. Of them. Of this place. Of teaching lifers. Once, I accidentally shook it and it didn't go off. So much for safety precautions.

I make my way into the classroom. The door opens and locks behind me. Yes, I am locked in with them, without a guard. The classroom is a sanctuary, a glass bubble that interrupts the grimness of the rest of the prison. It is clean and bright, lined with textbooks and aging computers, rows and rows of empty desks and a Smartboard that actually works. Ironically, the classroom is nicer, better-equipped, anyway, than the one I teach in at my expensive, elite, liberal arts college. Still, it is in a prison. Ashwin Manthripragada (2018) wisely reminds us:

> Although our goal is to recreate the college classroom and offer the
> students the opportunity to set mind, if not foot, into college, the

parameters of prison nevertheless delineate a distinct environment from the college campus. The unique parameters of the prison class-room thus determine education. (p. 71)

Nonetheless, the goal of this prison classroom is not unlike the goal of most college or university classrooms: to provide opportunities for intellectual growth, self-efficacy, and even intellectual freedom. And the teaching, as many who have ventured to teach "behind the wire" suggest, is an extraordinary privilege. In *College in Prison*, Daniel Kar-powitz (2017) writes:

> To this day, the approach to a prison building and the journey through its labyrinth of hallways are oppressive experiences. . . . But the classroom spaces themselves, created wherever I have the plea-sure of joining students in their college work, remain as gratifying as any good learning encounter anywhere. (p. 8)

Classes are a rare commodity and are always in high demand. The men learn about the classes through postings and announcements made by the education director. If they are interested in taking the class, they send the education director an internal memo, or "kite." The educa-tion director then determines who should be in the class by making certain the men are all currently in good standing (not on any kind of disciplinary watch) and that all have a high school diploma or equiv-alent. Usually more men sign up than there is room in the class, and I find myself allowing up to thirty students, knowing full well that over the course of our time together, a few will disappear—through natural attrition, disciplinary infractions, or transfer to another institution.

For this class, twenty-five men file in for class, one residential block at a time. They dress up, too, wearing the best versions of their prison garb, the cleanest blue denim shirts and "mom pants," the least-frayed gray sweatshirts. It's a sign of respect; whether it's for me or for the opportunity to learn, I can't say.

To date, I have taught 150 incarcerated men, ages eighteen to sixty-five, the majority of whom are serving life sentences. Of those, two-thirds were incarcerated while they were still juveniles. When

I began teaching I made a decision not to learn anything about the crimes my students had been convicted of. It's easy to find out. Like almost all departments of corrections, my state has an online database. You enter the person's name or "Offender ID number" and his crime, location of offense, and length of sentence pops up, along with a mug shot. I decided that if my stance toward them as a teacher was not to be affected in any way by their status as incarcerated people, then I needed to know them as students and not as criminals. Although I hadn't quite thought through it at the time, this was my first gesture toward considering education as both rehumanization and a step toward rewriting the narrative of self. Incarceration depends on a system of dehumanization.

Author Bryan Stevenson, in the documentary *13th*, states that criminalization is the opposite of humanization (DuVernay, 2016). In volunteer training, we are instructed to always refer to students as offenders, as if the only salient aspect of their entire personhood is their crime. And, in some ways within the penal system as it is currently constructed, it is. Yet I am reminded of what one of my formerly incarcerated students, Willie X Lloyd, once said, "Everyone's better than the worst they've ever done." I have that on my office door at my college. It replaced a witticism by John Dewey.

In describing his teaching at a maximum-security prison, Ashwin Manthripragada (2018) writes, "As teachers in the prison setting, we encounter prisoners foremost as students. We teach them to see themselves as serving out more than their sentence" (p. 86). So I choose to access the incarcerated people I teach simply as students, and I have come to realize that I may very well be the only person in their lives whose knowledge of them and interactions with them are not framed by their crime or by their status as an incarcerated person. It is a gift perhaps to both of us. I know that it is flawed by a kind of naivete that the guards are well aware of. It may indeed be possible to overnormalize the situation, to forget that my classroom, like all classrooms, is affected by the moods and relative states of well-being (or lack thereof) of all of the students, regardless of the context. I sometimes forget that my classroom is tinted with the pastels of despair, posttraumatic stress, sleeplessness, anxiety, and, yes, even mental illness. In my haste not to label any of them as criminals, thieves, murderers, sociopaths, even psychopaths, I eliminate the real possibility that in some cases, their background might have some useful explanatory power. "Know your students," I tell my college students who are preparing to be teachers, but here in the prison, I am, in some fundamental ways, ignoring my own advice. Still, I prefer to overcorrect this way, to err on the side of overestimation than to be a thoughtless addition to the machinery that continues to demean and dehumanize them.

Our prison classroom, then, becomes a kind of oasis, or a glass bubble that floats fragilely in this sea of indignity. For two hours a week, the "offenders" are transformed into writers, readers, and thinkers in ways that help them reshape their sense of themselves. The warden once told me that there is more civility on the cellblocks when the men are attending classes. Liberal arts education isn't designed to be a handmaiden to incarceration, but perhaps there is indeed a way it can counter prison's dehumanizing effects, by reminding us all of the humanity and intelligence that lies, in suspended animation, behind bars.

"How to Do a Full Body Workout in Your Cell"; Or, Lesson Planning in Prison

An important element of any educational psychology class is learning to create lesson plans. My educational psychology class in my prison class was no different. In addition to a longer unit plan, which I will discuss in a later blog entry, students were required to create and present a 10-minute lesson to their classmates. They also had the opportunity to work in pairs.

This assignment was a perfect example of how context shapes content.

For the most part, the student's lesson plans were marked by some aspect of their incarceration, even though the assignment didn't require them to do so. Kirby demonstrated how to be safe when welding, his MINNCOR job; Matthew discussed how to get grants for correspondence college courses while incarcerated; and LaVon and Ronald teamed up to demonstrate Texas Hold 'Em, a common pastime in the cellblock.

Of particular note was Leon, who ingeniously had created an entire workout program that can be completed entirely in one's cell. The class was completely captivated, especially as he demonstrated his push-ups, biceps bulging triumphantly.

Perhaps most poignantly, Luis gave a lesson on how to be a better parent even when one is incarcerated. Luis had contacted the Big Brother program to secure a mentor for his ten-year-old son. In fact, his gesture was featured in a recent article in our local newspaper.

However, the image that lingers most for me is Ronnie's lesson. He decided to teach origami.

Ronnie passed out colored origami paper and patiently explained how to make a paper bird. Bent in concentration, brows sweating, the blue-clad heavily tattooed tough guys fussed over their birds, becoming exasperated when the wings didn't lie just so.

"I really want mine to look like a bird, Ronnie. Can you help me?" "Can I have some extra paper?" "Can we do this during the break?" The fact that Ronnie's lesson had nothing at all to do with any aspect of incarceration made us all almost giddy.

As his lesson ended, Ronnie noticed the pathetic shape of my bird. "No offense but that's awful," he laughed. "Here, I'll make you one. It's the least I can do for you. Maybe," he says, "it's the only thing I can do for you."

He deftly folds a piece of colored paper into a bird, and I thank him. Right then, the guard comes, and the class ends unceremoniously as it always does, but this time 24 prisoners clutch colored birds on their way back to their cells.

Photo by Deborah Appleman

CHAPTER THREE

Of Freire and Frost

READING THE WORLD BEHIND BARS

I N THE FIRST CLASS I ever taught at the prison, Introduction to Literature, Doppler raised his hand in the middle of a class discussion.

"Hey, have you ever heard of this dude, Paulo Freire?" Had I ever heard of Paulo Freire, the famed Brazilian educator and philosopher, often credited with being a founder of critical pedagogy and liberatory education? Was I, a career educator in my fourth decade of teaching and training teachers, familiar with his approach to education? Of course I had heard of him—studied him, read him, even taught his works as bedrock or foundational reading, a sort of catechism of educational studies.

"Yes, as a matter of fact, I have. Have *you* read him?" I asked in astonishment.

"Yes," he replied, "and here's what I want to say. You teach that way. I mean, you teach like he said; you teach to liberate."

"Well, thanks," I replied sheepishly. "I think that's the best compliment I have ever gotten."

"I am not sure if it's a compliment or a curse," he replied, grinning broadly. "You are fucking me up . . . bad. How are we supposed to be liberated, how are our minds supposed to be freed, when we can't even take a shit without someone telling us it's time to get up? You want our minds to be free but the rest of us isn't, so how is that supposed to work? Tell me, teacher, how? How do I come into this classroom as a free thinker when I am not a free man?"

There, in a nutshell, lies the tension between education, at least the aims of it, and incarceration, or at least the stated purpose of it. The purpose of liberal arts education, after all, is to liberate. For centuries, philosophers have ruminated on the aims of education.

While there is clearly no consensus on the specific utilitarian purposes of education, most observers agree that it is to help realize the full potential of human beings, to help them more fully realize their humanness. Others comment on the ways in which education can help develop character or provide a moral compass by offering exemplars of moral thinking and reasoning. In an often-quoted student paper of 1947, Martin Luther King Jr. described a "two-fold function of education, both a utilitarian and a moral reason":

> The function of education, therefore, is to teach one to think intensively and to think critically. But education which stops with efficiency may prove the greatest menace to society. The most dangerous criminal may be the man gifted with reason, but with no morals.

He continues:

> We must remember that intelligence is not enough. Intelligence plus character—that is the goal of true education. . . . The broad education will, therefore, transmit to one not only the accumulated knowledge of the race but also the accumulated experience of social living. (1947)

This last sentiment echoes the perspective of noted educational philosopher John Dewey:

> Since education is not a means to living, but is identical with the operation of living a life which is fruitful and inherently significant, the only ultimate value which can be set up is just the process of living itself. (1916, p. 281)

Considering these perspectives on the nature and aims of education, the paradox of offering educational opportunities in prison, especially to those serving long or life sentences, is fraught in several ways. As Ashwin Manthripragada (2018) points out, "An embrace of the basic tools of language and writing and thinking means finding freedoms of thought and expression behind bars despite the consistent policing of physical bodies and prohibition on virtual bodies. The body that remains can think thoughts and complete assignments that are protected from scrutiny by security guards" (p. 75).

If the purpose of education is to offer pragmatic tools for living, then what use is it for those who will not be in the outside world again to use those skills? If the purpose of education is to help one find life's meaning, both spiritual and intellectual, then what chance does it have of being realized in such a seemingly hopeless environment? And, if the purpose of education is to make sure, as Martin Luther King asserted, that human beings are decent, behave decently, and do not become criminal, then what can education do for those who have already become criminal? Is it too late? Or then does its purpose become to rehabilitate, to correct the moral compass? Given these paradoxes, one may wonder what kind of education might best serve those behind bars for the duration of their life. What is the life of the mind like behind bars and what does that tell us about what kind of education to offer?

One indication of the nature of the life of the mind behind bars is found in the products of intelligence that occur without a particular educational structure to prompt or guide them. For example, one can examine the art, writing, and publications such as newsletters or newspapers that the incarcerated initiate and maintain on their own. The prison newspaper was begun, legend has it, by the Younger Brothers of Jesse James's gang after their ill-fated bank robbery in Northfield, Minnesota. It has been running continuously ever since. Generations of convicted felons have served as the editors, upholding its origins as a prisoner-run paper. A cursory glance at a typical issue of *The Prison Mirror* offers a peek into the intellectual life of the prison. There is usually a lead article, often something about prison life or conditions. There are impassioned editorials, whose subjects range from the cost of phone calls to prison food to an analysis of some aspect of the prison-industrial complex. There are also articles about social aspects of life on the inside, such as parenting in prison or the possibility of conjugal visits. Interviews, conducted by the editors of the newspaper, are often included. Those interviews can focus on political leaders, such as the governor or a mayor, Department of Corrections personnel, including the warden and associate warden, or former prisoners who have "made it" on the outside. In every issue, at least two or three artists are featured, with elaborate charcoal or pen-and-ink drawings filling up entire pages. Creative writing, often poems or sometimes short stories, also appear. Regular articles about restorative justice appear as an indication of the prisoners' constant, relentless thinking about their crimes.

There is also an acute political sensibility that is visible in the newspaper and in the classes I teach, one that points to another irony or paradox. These incarcerated men, who produce such thoughtful pieces of creative work, are both in this world and not of this world. They are literally disenfranchised, having lost the right to vote—a disenfranchisement that extends, in most states, to even after they are released. I remember in the last election being startled by a big sign that said, "If you are a felon or have recently been released, you can't vote here."

This is the kind of continued recriminalization even after release that Michelle Alexander (2010) and others refer to when they discuss mass incarceration as the new Jim Crow. In addition to voting, the stigmatization continues for finding employment and housing. The "ban the box" movement (referring to the yes/no check box next to the question "Have you ever been convicted of a felony?") is one way that some have tried to address this constant recriminalization. It is a reminder of the nearly permanent stigma and hurdles that make successful reentry so difficult and recidivism so insidiously likely.

Recently, I attended a reading cosponsored by a writers' collective and a group of writers on the outside who teach classes in the prison. So much of the work that the incarcerated writers read was political. Even Two-Tone, our resident clown and joker, produced a smart and scathing commentary on the Trumpian reality of the world, feeling as worried by the prospect of a nuclear holocaust as an everyday citizen. Why shouldn't he be? He may be walled away from this world, but he is still very much a part of it. Perhaps one of the goals of education behind bars is to make more permeable the walls that separate these men from the world they continue to analyze, question, and reimagine.

Daniel Karpowitz (2017), founder of the Bard Prison Initiative, which helps provide liberal arts education for the incarcerated, notes that students in prison

> undertake a personal struggle to rekindle or realize their own long-deferred or thwarted ambitions, and they commit to caring for and building something precious, despite being surrounded by an institution that mostly evokes resistance, cynicism, and alienation. . . . Indeed the very circumstances that confront the student in prison often lead to a greater awareness of the stakes involved in pursuing education, and a more profound fulfillment of liberal learning's promise by a wider range of students. . . . These conditions make the academic and personal achievements of students in prison all the more remarkable; they also deepen, rather than compromise, the importance of the liberal arts as a mode of education acutely relevant to the prison and the students within it. (pp. 4–5)

Sound educational practices spring from the resources and interests that students bring to the classroom. Thus, as a teacher, I pay close attention to the intellectual gestures that exist outside of the classroom so that I can create a classroom that will be responsive to my students' interests, needs, and abilities. This is true for all of my teaching, but it seems especially important in crafting classes for the incarcerated, who live most of the time in an environment that is not conducive to learning. In what follows, I offer some examples of the kind of intellectual activities in which the students engage, what this reveals about the domains of intellectual inquiry that are relevant to the incarcerated, and how education can help to transform the social fabric within the prison. Also, it is all too easy to underestimate the intellectual powers of the incarcerated, to, in a way, infantilize them. Perhaps it's because of the undeniable range of ability. My incarcerated students typically include newly minted GEDs taking their first college course and experienced students who have already earned four-year degrees, some on the outside and some on the inside.

The first course I ever taught in a prison, the one where Doppler inquired about Paulo Freire, was called Introduction to Literature, a bread-and-butter standard for any liberal arts course of study. In this course, students read both contemporary and classic texts. In addition, the students were introduced to the concept of reading texts from multiple critical literary perspectives (Appleman, 2016). The central purpose of this approach to teaching literature, as I have argued elsewhere (Appleman, 2001, 2009, 2015, 2016), is twofold: first, to help students learn to read—and, if necessary, to resist—the ideology that is inscribed in texts. For example, an astute reader should detect the colonialism in *A Passage to India*, the misogyny in *Lolita*, or the feminism in *Pride and Prejudice*. The other equally important goal is to have readers learn to inhabit multiple perspectives as they consider a single text and by doing so, perhaps become less dogmatic or, at least, less dualistic in their thinking.

While this approach to reading literary texts has always been significant to me, the context of the prison made these intellectual aims even more salient and, in some ways, both dangerous and counterintuitive. One of the aims of reading with multiple perspectives is to help students understand the perspective of others. In an increasingly diverse world, this seems to be a desirable skill not just for intellectual purposes but for social purposes as well. The prison is a deeply divided and segregated place. I was warned early on to revise my usual pedagogical methods of assembling the class into randomly assigned small groups. There are rivalries and histories, bad blood between prisoners; you can't put them blindly into groups, I was told.

The divisions in the prison and in my classroom are racial, cultural, social, and educational. There is animus, racial and otherwise. Would learning to read from a variety of critical perspectives help ease the divide between warring factions of the prison population? That seems too much to ask for, but at the very least, there is some evidence that the students in my class became, in the words of William Perry, much more relativistic in their thinking.

For example, this Introduction to Literature class had a lively discussion of Robert Frost's "The Road Not Taken," a poem I frequently use to illustrate the plausibility of more than one point of view. What did each road represent? Which road should the speaker have taken? In that discussion, and in subsequent discussions, students quickly began to admit the possibility that there was more than one possible and valid interpretation of a text. They began to listen more carefully to dissenting opinions. They began to name the ideologies (in this case, rugged individualism and nonconformity) that spawn a particular interpretation. They began to become careful readers and critical thinkers. Together, we tackled texts that were inflected with issues of race, gender, and class. We read James Baldwin, Richard Wright, Toni Morrison, Ta-Nehisi Coates. The passion continued, but so did the civility. I started experimenting with small groups, and they started to learn from one another.

As with other readers, using critical lenses helps students read the world as well as the word (yes, Doppler, it *is* about Paulo Freire). This intellectual tool is powerful and helps unmask the ideology inherent in texts and contexts. Reading and, if necessary, resisting ideology can help students have more control over their environment. They can read the intent inscribed in texts, especially if messages are intended to control them.

Although it seems fruitful to read the sexism in a sitcom or the social class bias in an advertisement in the *New York Times Sunday Magazine*, reading the ideology of the controlled environment of the prison might seem less productive. What kinds of skills or predispositions are needed to be able to survive in prison? Is it better to have a clear and painful sense of the ideology and understand it or to be blissfully oblivious to it? No wonder Doppler is mad at me. This education may be making his incarceration less tolerable as it makes him feel simultaneously both more powerful and more powerless. Again, we are faced with the tension that haunts my prison teaching, the seemingly irresoluble contradiction between education as freeing and incarceration as confining. Yet, there seems, on balance, to be something immeasurably valuable when the incarcerated are engaged in opportunities to animate their intelligence . . . and to reassert their humanity.

Noting that college and prison "have very different objectives and cannot, in fact, be reconciled," Daniel Karpowitz (2017) asserts that with proper attention to the differences in institutional character and mission, a "person in prison may live, with great power and purpose, a life approximating that of a student" (p. 97). Another prison teacher in a correctional facility in New York asked her incarcerated students what being in a college classroom revealed about who they were.

> They told me it meant they were courageous, creative, committed knowledge-seekers, that they were determined to make something of themselves while doing time. . . . It meant that they were resilient and able to lift themselves above the daily horror of life in prison. (Kunen, 2017, p. 27)

One evening, when the class has been dismissed by the guards, and the men are ordered back into their cells, Ross and I walk together for part of the way. Ross is mercurial, temperamental, highly opinionated, and a passionate learner. He uses any opening he can in any class, regardless of the subject or topic, to rage against his favorite topic, the prison-industrial complex. He is the kind of incessant class participant who makes others in the class roll their eyes with weary impatience, as if to say, "we have heard this all before," and they have.

Ross gets into trouble with greater frequency than almost any other student I have had. In the first course he took, his classroom attendance was made irregular by his frequent visits to segregation, or what the men call "the hole," where prisoners are sent after what is deemed a serious disciplinary infraction. During this most recent class, his third, he hasn't yet been sent to the hole.

"You know," he begins softly, so that we can't be overheard. (I am not sure if it's the guards or his fellow students from whom he wants to keep this admission.) "I feel as if this education is both awakening my brain but taming my anger."

"How so?" I ask, surprised.

"I don't know. I feel as if I am being forced to think, to be rational for the first time in my life, and that is keeping me from acting out. I don't want to get thrown into the hole, because then I would miss class. And I also, for the first time, am trying to see things from another perspective, like we did with those theories in Introduction to Literature. You remember? Our first class. I think you called them critical lenses."

I nod vigorously.

"So, thanks, I guess, is what I am saying." He stops and turns to me, but we are admonished to keep moving by the guard who is right behind us. "Thanks for coming in. I can actually feel myself becoming a better person. Isn't that what education is all about?"

Martin Luther King would agree.

Deborah Appleman with students doing group work. *Photo by Tim Eling*

Tony and the Blue Book

Tony is a tough guy. Real tough. For the life of me, I can't imagine most of my students doing anything violent. They look innocent—young and fresh-faced, and actually sweet. No kidding. Tony isn't one of those guys. He looks mean.

His eyes don't smile, even when his mouth does. His hair is close-cropped, and his face is etched with lines of fatigue and resignation, though I can sometimes catch, in a rare flash of a grin, traces of how handsome he once was.

Tony's arms ripple with tattooed muscles. He works in industry, not like so many of my students who work as tutors. He isn't afraid to dive into our spirited and inevitably racially marked discussions, standing up for the "white is right" side (a blog-worthy topic on its own) and calling out everyone, including me, on what he calls our "politically correct bullshit." Tony told me early on that he was a "lifer." I asked him not to tell me more.

So you can imagine my surprise when during our in-class educational psychology midterm, Tony panicked and cried. I had given the students all of the questions for the midterm one week ahead of time and told them that the exam would be open-note and open-book to force up the higher levels of Bloom's taxonomy. Bloom insisted that facts were at the lower level of cognitive understanding, while application, synthesis, and evaluation were what he called "higher level thinking." Allowing students to use their notebooks forces the teacher to ask questions that don't require mere recall or memorization.

The exam is very similar to the ones I use in the educational psychology class I teach every year at Carleton College. I often give it as a take-home exam. Take-home exams don't work in a prison setting. The cell is not a dorm room;

it is a cage, designed to confine human beings. The cellblocks are subject to lockdowns, potential confiscation of material, and other unpredictable interruptions designed to ensure security. You can't count on quality study time in the cellblock. Some "offenders" have access to computers; some don't. Some have typewriters; some don't. So, in order to level the playing field, as it were, I have everyone write the exam in class.

On the day of the exam, I passed out blue books, invited the students to spread out their notes and outlines, and started keeping time on our Smartboard. Then, as is my customary practice, I walked around the classroom, checking to see how everyone was doing and if anyone had any questions to whisper to me.

When I got to Tony, I stopped short. His arms were folded, his blue book was closed, and his eyes were wet. I crouched down next to him. "'Sup, Tony?"

"I can't do this," he whispered hoarsely, and a tear spilled out of his steely eyes.

"Come with me," I replied.

We sprinted out of the classroom into the hallway. The officer on duty glanced at us quizzically and then seemed to immediately know that he should look away.

"I just can't do this. This test is scaring the shit out of me. I almost didn't come tonight. I wanted to bag the whole class. No offense," he added quickly. "I really liked it up to now. But I'm afraid I'm gonna flunk the exam."

"Tony, don't worry. You won't flunk it, and even if you did, you could still pass the class; this exam is only worth twenty percent of the course grade and you've gotten B's and B+'s on your papers. You can make it up."

"Well," he said, "I came because my daughter just started college, and she's taking a class like this too. I thought that for once we could do something at the same time, like doing it together. I can't let her down, not any more than I already have." The tears are falling now, for both of us.

"Tony," I said, "here's the plan. Go back in there, open the blue book and pretend to write anything. After the first person turns it in, then you do the same.

Then no matter how you did on the test, we'll figure out how you can still pass the class by kicking major butt on your lesson plan."

"Okay," he mumbled, as we returned to the classroom.

Later on that evening, I opened Tony's blue book. It only had five words sprawled across two pages in shaky cursive:

"Thank you. I'll be back."

When I told this story to my colleague Bill Titus, he remarked, "Have you ever thought of having them write their exams on something other than a blue book? Maybe it's simply the format that makes people anxious." Smart guy.

Like many of the lessons I've learned as a prison teacher, this one has some relevance to Carleton students as well. Perhaps there is a kind of operant conditioning at work here, one that make students' palms sweat and hearts beat faster at the site of a blue book. I even found some research on this (Schworm, 2008).

Maybe it's time to rethink using blue books in any class, ever.

In the meantime, I am happy to report that Tony stayed with the class and rocked his lesson plan and presentation. When he got his grade on the lesson, I caught a glimpse of that elusive dimpled grin.

CHAPTER FOUR

"No Hugs for Thugs"
SURVEILLANCE AND CONTROL

H IS MOTHER DIED SUDDENLY. He is an only child, incarcerated at the age of twenty-one for 25 years. Both his father and his grandmother, who wrote him letters every day, died during his incarceration. Although he was allowed to see his father's body, he was not allowed to attend the funeral. He was a student in the first prison class I ever taught and quickly became my most distinguished, winning writing award after writing award, coming to the attention of folks like Joyce Carol Oates and Jimmy Santiago Baca.

His mother was his lifeline, the only one left after friendships faded, loves were lost, and other family members passed away. She was an oasis of humanity in his desert of incarceration, lush with unconditional love and fierce advocacy. She visited him three times a week, writing impassioned letters to whichever warden happened to be in charge, plumping his account with money so he could make phone calls and buy items at the canteen, and trying, as best as she could, to make him feel loved and well-parented.

It wasn't easy, given the tremendous constraints placed on human relationships, even mother-child relationships, by the correctional system. She would often say, "I have to remind myself that I am not the one who is incarcerated, even though I feel like I am."

I got to know her well as he wrote his book, one that was published by a distinguished university press and went on to become a finalist for a nonfiction book award. We pored over his manuscript together, met with his editor and publisher, sent notes to the typist, and frequently exchanged good wishes and thumb drives. I came to admire the way in which she transformed her love for her only child, her incarcerated son, into a passion for prison reform. She was a force of nature and reared like a mama bear when her son experienced both unexpected and expected indignities of incarceration such as when the mail room "lost" his newly ordered glasses, or when he lay writhing in excruciating pain on his cell floor, trying to pass a kidney stone as corrections officers passed by, ignoring his cries for help.

His mother dropped dead unexpectedly, at the age of sixty-seven, and with her, his most significant human connection dropped out of the universe. Within hours of the discovery of her death, I got word from a mutual acquaintance both of her passing and of his desire to see me. But I knew protocol forbade me from visiting prisoners as long as I was teaching within the system. It seemed inhumane to ignore his plea and to leave him alone in his grief. But it also seemed like a great deal to risk, the possibility that I might not be able to continue teaching in the prison if I were caught. I tried to think of what his mother would want me to do. She always warned me to be careful and not risk my work. "Let other people agitate," she would say. "The most radical thing you can do is to keep teaching." Still, I didn't know what to do.

This conundrum, whether to visit my former student and risk my standing with the Department of Corrections or leave him stranded in a prison cell in his grief, seemed to capture the tensions that arise when teaching—perhaps the most potentially humane of interactions—occurs in an inhumane situation. How can we offer those gestures of empathy that are at the very heart of teaching when the context of the institution in which we are teaching forbids us to do so?

I contend that the culture of surveillance invades the culture of the prison classroom and seriously limits the degree to which truly productive student-teacher relationships can be formed. That limitation, in the end, also tamps down the level of transformation and intellectual liberation that can be achieved. While the sudden death of my student's mother is the most dramatic personal challenge I have faced, there have been others as well.

Ten years ago, during the very first course I taught in the prison, one of the most promising students in the class was sent to "the hole," for staying a few minutes too long in the shower. A lifer, incarcerated at seventeen for a gang-related crime with a 99+25-year sentence, he later explained that sometimes he had to exercise, in small and seemingly inconsequential gestures such as lingering in the shower, whatever was left of his "free will" in order not to lose himself completely. A dedicated student and a gifted writer, he managed to receive—from his cellblock mates who were also in the class—and complete all of the assignments, even though he missed the rest of the course. As I was leaving the prison on the last night of class, he positioned himself by the entry to his cellblock and, with the permission of the cluster of guards nearby, thrust a folder of his completed work into my hands.

Overwhelmed by his diligence and commitment to learning, all of my usual teacherly gestures of warmth and positive reinforcement kicked in, and I momentarily forgot to remember where I was. I accepted the packet enthusiastically, lavished him with praise, and . . . gave him a hug. He stood impassively, arms at his sides, and offered a wry smile.

The next day, I received a phone call from the warden, who sternly reminded me that no physical contact whatsoever, not even gestures of approval, were allowed. The warden was kind, but firm: I was on probation, and my student was back in the hole.

In another incident, an incarcerated student called me at home to double-check on his credits for a particular class he had taken with me. He was working toward his associate's degree and the class hadn't shown up yet on his transcript. Unbeknownst to either of us, all of his phone calls were being recorded, and the phone call to me was brought to the attention of the education director of the facility, a particularly generous and highly regarded educator, respected by prisoners and corrections personnel alike.

"I know you didn't discuss anything you weren't supposed to," she admitted rather sheepishly, "but you didn't report him."

Report him? And make his miserable life even more miserable? How could I ever bring myself to do that, I wondered, as I lamely replied that I didn't know I was supposed to report him.

"Well, you won't be banned this time, but he can never take a class with you again."

A month later, as I was entering the classroom to teach a class on the personal essay, we passed each other in the narrow hallway, with a guard positioned at each end. I wanted to say something to him to let him know that the denial of the privilege of teaching him was perhaps nearly as painful to me as not being able to enroll in a class was to him. We caught each other's eyes. His welled up with tears. I looked away and walked solemnly into a room full of waiting students who had observed the brief interaction but were puzzled by it. "Too bad about Eli," one student mumbled. "I know he was trying like hell to get into this class."

These incidents illustrate the ways in which the constraints of control in prison are, in the end, constraints that are placed on the student-teacher relationship. While they may seem individually insignificant, their cumulative effect weighs heavily on both teachers and students. More than the subject that is being taught, the quality of educational experiences is in many ways largely determined by the quality of the student-teacher relationship. For many of us teachers, that relationship is sacred in its purity, nearly holy in its intent. Thus, it is not surprising that the nature of the relationship between student and teacher has been explored from spiritual and psychological perspectives.

The philosopher and theologian Martin Buber (who was notably committed to adult education initiatives even in the middle of the last century) reminds us of the centrality of the establishment of the "I-thou" relationship in fostering the kind of dialogue that he considers to be essential to authentic learning. Dialogue in the Buberian sense is not simply classroom talk; it is what happens when each individual—the teacher and the student—meets and regards the other with openness, with ethical intent, and with engagement. He writes:

> [T]he teacher must really *mean* him as the definite person he is in his potentiality and his actuality; more precisely, he must not know him as a mere sum of qualities, strivings and inhibitions, he must be aware of him as a whole being and affirm him in this wholeness. (1958, pp. 164–65)

Similarly, Parker Palmer writes eloquently of the act of teaching as one that is dependent on the connection between a teacher and her students. For Palmer, that connection is made between the heart of the teacher and the heart of a student. As he explains:

> The connections made by good teachers are held not in their methods but in their hearts—meaning *heart* in its ancient sense, as the place where intellect and emotion and spirit and will converge in the human self.
>
> As good teachers weave the fabric that joins them with students and subjects, the heart is the loom on which the threads are tied, the tension is held, the shuttle flies, and the fabric is stretched tight. Small wonder, then, that teaching tugs at the heart, opens the heart, even breaks the heart—and the more one loves teaching the more heartbreaking it can be. The courage to teach is the courage to keep one's heart open in those very moments when the heart is asked to hold more than it is able so that teachers and students and subject can be woven into the fabric of community that learning, and living, require. (1999, p. 11)

It is these very connections, at the root of good teaching and therefore at the root of a good education, against which the carceral system fortifies itself. To teach in a prison in a way that follows the rules, the heart must be disengaged from the act of teaching, but as Palmer so eloquently explains, that actually can't be done.

Mike Rose, one of the most astute observers of American education writing today, offers more evidence of the importance of the human connection, even, perhaps especially, as he chronicles what works for those given "second chances" at school. He emphasizes the central importance of the teacher-student relationship, especially for adult learners. He writes:

> Teachers can be instrumental in fostering help-seeking behavior. They can discuss this issue directly, providing anecdotes from their own and their past students' experiences. Teachers can ask to see students and make the appointment on the spot. Central to these

issues is the kind of atmosphere faculty create in their classrooms, that is, the sense students pick up from the way a teacher addresses them, responds to questions and deals with requests. Here's the bottom line for students: Is this a safe place, and do I feel respected? If the answer is yes, students will be more willing to answer or ask a question, participate and take a chance. . . . By seeing the role of teacher as providing an introduction not only to subject matter but to college life, by making the hidden visible, by being systematic in getting students to office hours and tutoring centers, by striking up a casual conversation and by just talking openly about the tricks of the trade, teachers can end up making a big difference in their students' lives. (2013)

Buber, Rose, Palmer, and other commentators on the nature of education consistently point out the centrality of the teacher-student relationship. Teachers don't simply teach subjects; they teach people. Every teacher worth her salt learns this lesson through challenges and resistance early on—whether it is a boisterous fourth grader, a sullen high school junior, a cynical college student, or a reluctant adult learner. A relationship between a teacher and her students becomes a gateway to the subject. And it isn't about the teacher, about any of those white-savior/teacher-as-hero motifs. No, it's about letting the learner know that you have an authentic interest in him and his learning, that he won't be exploited or misunderstand.

Herb Kohl, in *I Won't Learn from You* (1999), points out that the learning of some students, especially students who have been marginalized from school and society in innumerable ways, is actually impeded by the perception that the teacher is in a position of privilege, power, and control that could exploit the student. This perception, and the oppositional stance it can engender, can be exacerbated in a correctional setting if teachers are viewed as compliant and willing instruments of the mechanisms of incarceration. In *Right to Be Hostile*, Erica Meiners (2007) makes a similar point. Incarcerated students have often experienced a lifetime of hostile systems, systems of both education and incarceration that have consistently punished and isolated them. This prior experience and set of institutional expectations can make it particularly difficult for teachers and students to establish a trusting and productive relationship.

While there is a wide range of educational offerings in America's prisons, ranging from vocational training to a variety of postsecondary courses, most departments of corrections acknowledge the importance of educational opportunities through both their programming and their rhetoric. Still, there is a stiff set of regulations that chills and eventually attempts to impede the educational enterprise.

In the state where I teach, all volunteers for the Department of Corrections (DOC) submit yearly to a three-hour training session. The trainings are usually filled with folks on a religious mission; they wear broad smiles and wooden crosses around their necks and carry well-worn Bibles. In this group of well-meaning do-gooders, I feel as if both my skepticism and my agnosticism brands me right away as an outlier.

The session begins with the distribution of a 50-page booklet of instructions, prohibitions including everything from what to bring in to what to wear or, more accurately, what not to wear. We are told to always refer to the prisoners as "offenders," and to use that as the term of address—not Mr. Black, for example, but "Offender Black." This means that every interaction, every conversational exchange, is framed by a linguistic acknowledgment of the student's status as someone who has "offended," someone who has been found guilty of a crime.

We watch a video of a current prisoner who explains all the ways in which prisoners can manipulate or take advantage of volunteers. The Bible people nod solemnly. The corrections officer running the training then talks about how much each prisoner costs the our state each day to incarcerate and offers that some are there for "three hots and a cot." "I've known these guys for years," he says, "and you can't let your guard down. They may seem nice, and some of them actually are, but even the nice ones will take advantage of you. Also, please sign this release. It says, 'If you are taken hostage, we can't help you.' Thanks for coming and good luck."

From this orientation a tone of suspicion and surveillance is set. We appreciate you coming in here, they say, but we will be watching you. Closely.

In most education programs in correctional facilities, teacher-student interaction is strictly limited to the classroom. There can be no outside correspondence, communication, or visits. As long as one is actively teaching in one DOC facility, one cannot appear on the visiting list of anyone in any facility statewide. Heartfelt letters of gratitude, sometimes filled with pages and pages of new writing, go unanswered. It is hard to receive those letters and leave them unanswered, to get telephone calls and quickly hang up, knowing that such communication is prohibited and may well be recorded. Even though the students know these gestures of appreciation are forbidden, sometimes their gratitude wins out over their caution. It feels difficult, almost uncivil, to ignore them.

There is no opportunity for student conferences, no office hours, no individual attention. We can't bring in books we know our students would like, something that English teachers consider to be a central part of their teaching. All materials for the classroom need to be ordered well in advance, sent directly to the facility, and vetted by the correctional officers in the mail room. This restriction seriously limits the ability to change direction in a class, to bring in contemporaneous happenings, to weave together in real time the outside world with the inside world. This limitation also affects teachers' ability to bring in the tools of the trade to students, to offer them books, pencils, pens, notebooks. These items are viewed as potential vessels of contraband rather than potential vessels of renewal.

To be sure, there are reasons for the wariness of corrections officials and for the establishment of strict rules and procedures within a carceral space, one that exists for confined human activity. Every year some volunteer breaks a rule, brings in an illegal substance, violates the rules, crosses boundaries, even falls in love. There is no doubt that there is protocol that must be followed for the sake of safety and common sense. Still, the ubiquity of surveillance, of restrictions, both physical and otherwise, serves to constrain the degree to which the transcendent nature of educational experiences can take root and blossom into what could be important transformative relationships that could become the key to preserving the humanity of the incarcerated, not to mention improving opportunity for success on the outside for those who will eventually be released.

This illustrates a major source of tension in considering education for the incarcerated. The goals and aims of education and the goals and aims of incarceration are fundamentally opposite. Education seeks to liberate; incarceration necessarily seeks to constrain. Education seeks to humanize; incarceration inevitably seeks to dehumanize. Education seeks to give the individual power; incarceration only works if the incarcerated are rendered powerless. Yet departments of corrections are aware that education is the only reliable key to reduce recidivism. So how does one accomplish the education needed to retrain, rehabilitate, and heal while at the same time effectively controlling individuals until they are released?

If education is to be humanizing, then the students need to be treated with humanity. Ninety-three percent will return to society. They will carry the traces of their infantilization and their dehumanization with them back into the world. They will enter places where the "Have you been convicted of a felony" check box prevents them from voting, from renting, from being teachers, and from being hired for other jobs. If education is truly to break the cycle of incarceration, we need to be sure to retain the possibility of humane interactions between teachers and students in prison education programs, despite the contradictory learning landscapes we may encounter (Karpowitz, 2017).

Walking out of the prison recently with a visiting poet who was a new volunteer, I asked him how everything was going.

"Fine," he replied. "The guys are great, but the whole system is hard to get used to."

"Yes," I nodded vigorously in agreement. "Our students are not the only ones being surveilled. Welcome to the Panopticon!"

"What's that?" Michael asked, brow furrowed.

"You don't know what the Panopticon is?" I replied incredulously. "I don't think you can teach in a prison without knowing what it is. We are in it, with our students, and it will affect every gesture between us. Time to read some Foucault!"

Michael shrugged his shoulders in a way that made me wonder if perhaps he'd be better off not knowing.

Saying Goodbye to Grandma in Chains

Eddie comes up to me after the midterm and says he is afraid that he hasn't done as well as he should have. Eddie is a tutor, a sweet and serious man in his late twenties who works with other prisoners to help them earn their GEDs.

"You see, my grandma died this week," Eddie says. "And I was too sad to study."

"I'm so sorry, Eddie. Of course I understand."

"I did get to see her, though. They let me go see her."

"Wow, Eddie," I said, incredulous at the seemingly humanitarian gesture. "So you got to say goodbye to her?"

"Well, no. I waited till she died. I had a choice but I had to be in the orange jumpsuit all shackled and in chains. I didn't want her to see me like that; I didn't want that to be the last picture she had of me as she left this earth. So I waited till she died. They took me to the funeral home. And I kissed her goodbye."

CHAPTER FIVE

"I Will Write Myself Out of Prison"

REWRITING THE SELF

I T WAS THE EVENING OF THE READING for our Advanced Creative Writing class. "Public" readings were always a good final event for classes, and the incarcerated writers were each able to invite two of their fellow prisoners. A smattering of Department of Corrections personnel also attended—the education director and several instructors. Sometimes the associate warden or even the warden was in attendance.

This particular class reading featured the work of men with whom I had worked over several writing classes for nearly ten years. I had invited the commissioner of the Department of Corrections. A political appointee under our benevolent Democratic governor, this commissioner, unlike his predecessor, was kind and humane. He actually seemed to care about the incarcerated who were in his charge and seemed to have a more rehabilitative than punitive orientation. To my grateful surprise he came to the reading, greeting prisoners with a handshake and a hello as he made his way to the front of the room. He knew nearly all of them by name.

During the reading, I watched him from across the aisle as the writers shared their poetry, short stories, and memoirs, and performed a collaborative poem. His face reddened as he listened, and his eyes watered in appreciation, it seemed to me. At the end of the reading, he rose and walked over to the row of incarcerated writers and addressed them directly.

"I am moved, so deeply moved, by your words. I see sons, fathers, husbands, all in those words, and I can see how you have changed. That event that got you in here, it is in your past. It should be retreating into the rearview mirror. It is not who you are, and it does not define you. *This* is who you are. Your words define you. You have not given up on yourselves and we will not give up on you. Your words inspire me. Thank you for sharing them."

The writers looked almost dumbstruck as they tried to take in the significance of what the commissioner had said. The "incarcerator-in-chief" had told them that their crime was not what defined who they were. This was stunning, considering the myriad ways in which the system continued to recriminalize them, from insisting on the term "offender" to various daily indignities such as timed showers and exorbitantly expensive telephone rates. He also told them, indirectly perhaps, that their words were reshaping them. And it is this notion that literacy can recraft the identity of the incarcerated that this chapter explores.

There has been considerable research on the relationship between literacy and identity (Yagelsky, 2000). Sometimes "identity" research focuses on the ways in which writers adopt different voices for particular rhetorical situations. There is also a good deal of often optimistic research about the ways in which literacy can be a liberatory practice (Lockard and Rankins-Roberts, 2018). There is ample discourse about the ways in which higher education and writing "can transform the lives of those in prison" (Berry, 2017, p. 5). Berry also wisely warns us of the ways in which these hopeful narratives of transformation can be both simplistic and overly optimistic. He reminds us of the importance to "better understand the complexities of literate practice in various contexts, especially behind bars" (p. 6). He encourages those who are engaged in this work to "develop pedagogies that are untethered in naïve beliefs in literacy's power yet mindful of realistic possibilities as well as the work that can take place in the present moment" (p. 7).

These warnings are well heeded. There is much to say about the overromanticization and naivete of some well-intended discourse regarding the transformative power of literacy for the incarcerated. The realities of the carceral state and the prison-industrial complex are undeniable, perhaps even insurmountable. Words alone, even eloquent and eventually published words, won't dismantle that reality. As Berry and others have pointed out, a narrative of hope, one that positions literacy that can not only transform the individual but may also be regarded as "the cure for any societal ills" can be both simplistic and shortsighted (Berry, 2017, p. 6). In some ways, this optimistic trope of literacy as possibility can even feed into equally dangerous narratives about those teachers who offer literacy instruction to the marginalized and disenfranchised. Literacy teachers who enter into carceral spaces must be aware, regardless of their gender, of what Erica Meiners has dubbed the syndrome of "White Lady Bountiful," a kind of patronizing, colonial, and often raced orientation that may make literacy educators feel better about themselves but in the end is neither practical nor realistic for the incarcerated (Alexander, 2010; Meiners, 2007). In fact, this well-intended but unrealistic approach to literacy for the incarcerated may become almost cruel as it both minimizes and demeans the reality of incarcerated life while at the same time delivering false promises.

While there are clear limits and undeniable dangers to the narrative of hope and transformation for the incarcerated through literacy, I have witnessed its undeniable power to do just that. Through the lived experiences of the writers with whom I have worked over the last decade, there is no denying that writing can transform someone's sense of self. Perhaps that kind of individual rather than structural transformation is a more realistic way of thinking about "the power of literacy." It is not a large macro-narrative about social justice or political reform. Rather its focus is smaller in scope but, I would argue, equally stunning and momentous: changes that an individual experiences. I worry that the justified critiques of prison literacy initiatives (Berry, 2018) sometimes overlook the small but important moments in the face of larger theoretical concerns. Perhaps we need to limit our claims about the transformative power to a micro rather than a macro phenomenon, to the personal rather than the political. Nevertheless, as the old feminist slogan reminds us, the personal *is* political. Perhaps, in the end, there can be no more worthwhile endeavor than helping to create the conditions under which an individual can reclaim his sense of self and therefore his humanity.

Jimmy Santiago Baca (also cited by Berry) is perhaps the primary example of this kind of transformation. Formerly incarcerated in a brutal Arizona prison, Baca transformed himself from being nearly illiterate to becoming a major poet. In his work, my incarcerated students do find both hope and possibility, in part because his experience of incarceration is deeply woven into his craft. He writes:

> I culled poetry from odors, sounds, faces, and ordinary events occurring around me. Breezes bulged me as if I were cloth; sounds nicked their marks on my nerves; objects made impressions on my sight as if in clay. There, in the soft language, life centered and ground itself in me and I was flowing with the grain of the universe. Language placed my life experiences in a new context, freeing me for the moment to become with air as air, with clouds as clouds, from which new associations arose to engage me in present life in a more purposeful way. (2001, pp. 239–40)

For my students, Baca was not merely a distant symbol of possibility; he embodied their experiences, his brutal past as well as his lyrical yet hard-bitten prose of the present. He offered the possibility that one could become a writer in the world, not just a "prison writer." He engaged with their work, offered his approval and encouragement, and wrote the foreword to an anthology of their creative work, writing:

> So these expressions of poetry and prose come as a great relief for me because these young ones seem to defy the order of the day. They are not mentored, they will mentor themselves. They are not given opportunity, they will make their own. They are given no future, they craft their own out of deep felt words carefully set into sentences that made poems that redefine their souls to the world beyond the walls of their confinement.

Their lives like weeds break the concrete steps leading to drug houses. Their voices shatter the screams, the convulsing tears, the silence of graveyards, and cry for respect, demand attention, strip away the deception of official double-speak, and look the reader straight in the eyes and say, Listen to me, I have something to say.

I have listened and your words have made my life even more connected to yours. (2009, p. 13)

Yet, as Baca and other formerly incarcerated writers would concede, transformation isn't alchemy; the traces of former selves and experiences are not completely vanquished. Deeds and misdeeds, broken hearts and promises, failed yet not forgotten relationships haunt the men in the present like vengeful ghosts. For me, and for my incarcerated students, these regretful reminders of the past temper the narrative arc of hope and possibility for the future into a more realistic projection.

Despite both the theoretical critiques and the real-world correctives, I have seen this transformation of self too often to let my well-informed academic skepticism prevail. For one of my students, Zeke, writing has become a core part of his identity. Zeke is an unusually gifted writer who has won several national writing awards and has recently published his memoir with a university press. He says:

Prior to my incarceration there was nothing to write for. I always felt like I would write a book one day, but I lived in a mental state where I could barely concentrate long enough to study for a driver's test, let alone imagine and edit any kind of long-form material. I still had no idea what sort of book I might write; it was probably mostly just an avenue that came from a starving ego. Getting locked up meant looking at my life as a sort of pause from the speed I had been accustomed to moving. It made me feel like I still wanted a sort of relevancy to my life, even if it was going to be short or difficult, and I resolved that one of the only ways that could ever be possible was if I left some sort of artistic expression in the universe. While others expressed themselves through other forms of visual art, the written word was the only expression I had.

Writing has become an essential part of who I see myself to be. Being a writer means I can speak for myself. I am also able to speak for those in similar situations and express themes in the world that are perplexing or unjust or that support notions of those whose voices don't get listened to or acknowledged. It has also meant my inclusion within a body of human existence that has been around forever, that framed the world in terms people could see as something other than what existed in their time. It also means something grew up in me. I started somewhere and was able to work my way into someone with a sharper grasp of what he could do. Coming from someone that never completed anything and without any kind of vision of who that person could be, I became someone capable of writing my own universe. Writers are active voices, sometimes even beyond their own lifetimes—and very realistically, it gave me an identity beyond the titles I was given when the judge dropped his gavel and an offender identification number was ironed over my name.

In prison, education exists in its purest form. There is no external payoff, no job, no material change in circumstances, and often no degree. For the most part, it seems that those who undertake education in prison do so for the purest of reasons: they want to learn for learning's sake and to experience the personal transformation that usually accompanies education at its best. Inevitably, this desire to transform, to become a better and sometimes different person, alters the personal narratives of those in prison. This change in personal narrative, in self-definition, is one of the most important aspects of the role of education in prison. For those who will reenter society after being incarcerated, their success and well-being depend largely on their ability to imagine themselves as more than felons, as more than criminals.

. . .

This ability to craft an alternate identity is equally crucial for those who will remain incarcerated. Liberal arts education offers alternative narratives to those who have defined themselves only by their current circumstances and by what they have done wrong. Echoing the commissioner's words, one student said, "I am more than what I did twenty years ago. I am a man with hopes and dreams, regrets and aspirations. I have a soul, a mind, and yes, a heart, even if society doesn't believe me. I hope my writing will convince them otherwise."

Zeke underscores this point:

> Education made me a writer, a student, a man, an individual outside statistics hidden somewhere. It made me a better son, able to replant seeds over the things I tore down a long time ago. It made me a voice that could articulate what I felt about myself and about this whole experience instead of just a projection of these emotions and feelings. It also made me understand what I could about the future, no matter how difficult it may still seem.

The power of literacy through writing is both important and well-documented. In his writer's statement, Ross wrote, "I will write my way out of prison." While some may view this as one of those impossible and unrealistic tropes of the narrative of hope, I have actually seen the ways in which literacy impacts incarceration.

Eli received a life sentence for first-degree murder at the age of fifteen. His is one of the few of my students' crimes with which I am familiar. A traveling carnival worker, he was involved in an altercation that resulted in the death of a fellow worker. He always uses the passive tense when he talks about the crime, in a way that obscures the degree of his own responsibility: "A man was killed," not "I killed a man." Like Baca, Eli entered prison semi-literate. Through GED courses as well as self-study, Eli learned to read and write. Then he began to study law.

Eli went through several lawyers as well as several unsuccessful appeals. At some point he rewrote his own appeal and succeeded in having his conviction overturned. After spending 17 years in prison, Eli is now free, working for the local ACLU chapter. He says that education is completely responsible for his freedom. He explains:

> Education is what freed me, there is no doubt about it. Funny thing is, it freed my mind long before my body was freed, and, to tell you the truth, that made incarceration harder to bear. But even in the darkest times, like the time there was a fire on the cellblock and my

cell literally was filled with smoke, I said to myself, I can't die like this. I need to make what I have learned matter, even if it is only to me. I am a much better man than I was when I came in, and it's because of education. And, because I learned to read and write critically, I was able to study and write my way out of prison.

Situated Communities of Practice

Usually, when we talk about transformation through education for the incarcerated, we consider individual stories, such as Zeke's or Eli's. Yet one of the most remarkable kinds of transformation in the prison is the rise of what Labe and Wenger (1991, 1998) call communities of practice. The incarcerated writers at the prison, thanks in large part to the support and encouragement of the nonprofit organization that offers creative writing classes throughout prisons in the state, have formed a writers' collective. This collective clearly meets Lave and Wenger's three criteria for a community of practice or CoP:

- **Mutual engagement:** Firstly, through participation in the community, members establish norms and build collaborative relationships; this is termed mutual engagement. These relationships are the ties that bind the members of the community together as a social entity.
- **Joint enterprise:** Secondly, through their interactions, they create a shared understanding of what binds them together; this is termed the joint enterprise. The joint enterprise is (re) negotiated by its members and is sometimes referred to as the "domain" of the community.
- **Shared repertoire:** Finally, as part of its practice, the community produces a set of communal resources, which is termed their shared repertoire; this is used in the pursuit of their joint enterprise and can include both literal and symbolic meanings.

There is some keen significance to the establishment and maintenance of this CoP in a prison. The CoP disrupts some of the structure of incarceration, including hierarchy, surveillance, and authority. The education department of the prison has granted the writers' collective a good deal of authority in deciding which writing classes should be offered, as well as when and who should be enrolled in the classes. A tutoring program has been established, so that the writers work side by side with the tutors. In one of the classes I recently taught the tutors were indispensable in a variety of ways. They circulated through the class during writing time, helping students with drafts. They provided useful insider knowledge about particular students that helped me modify course content to fit the needs of those learners, and they offered both sage advice and frank reviews of each class session. We met and conferred about the class as colleagues. I swear they began to see themselves with as much dignity as I saw them.

Some of the more advanced incarcerated writers have also transitioned from being tutors to becoming teachers, teaching beginning classes in creative writing. This opportunity to move from prisoner to writing student to tutor to writing teacher has had a profound effect on the identities, behavior, and self-narratives of the writers. They think of themselves first as writers with much to contribute to the communities in which they currently reside. And, for those who will be eventually released, it provides a foundation of self as well as a sense of skill and worth that will prove useful on the outside.

This CoP has also inverted some of the oppressive hierarchical structures in the prison. For example, the writers' collective serves as the editorial board for a facilities-wide journal, published yearly by a nonprofit organization that supports the teaching of creative writing in all of the correctional facilities in the state. The writer/teacher who is part of the editorial board, the only free member, organizes the meetings but functions more as an equal than as the arbiter. The collective also decided that it wanted to sponsor monthly readings that would feature writers from both the outside and the inside. Although it is fair to say that most of the organizing of those events is left up to staff and unincarcerated writers and teachers, the event itself feels like a remarkable toppling of the hierarchy inscribed in these spaces, with accomplished outside writers reading along incarcerated ones, both novice and accomplished. I sometimes like to close my eyes at these readings, shut out the prison blues, and realize that the quality of their writing and the passion with which they read make these writers indistinguish-able in talent from their free counterparts.

Chris, one of the founding members of the collective, said it best:

> For most of us, anything past family and friends were considered ene-mies or strangers. Our writing collective shapes community through shared interest and new ideas of social obligation; they are teaching us how to relate to people outside our natural bounds. In writing we find the opportunity to develop a bond with society through audi-ence. It's not simply about being heard, but about acknowledging the responsibility of listening. Through critiques, dissecting works, and public readings we are taught how to pay attention to the world around us. In doing this, we cannot help but discover the thread that binds us all together in this human condition.

Testimony of Transformation

In every writing class I teach, I ask students to compose a writer's state-ment, to help materialize what writing means to them and to offer evi-dence both to me and, more importantly, to themselves about the ways in which writing transforms their sense of self. In some ways I am asking them to say those things that go without saying, in the hope that the saying of them makes them more visible and perhaps more true. In these statements they frequently reflect on who they have been, who they hope to become, and how writing serves as a vehicle for that transformation. These statements also serve as a counterpoint to the generally justified cynicism and wariness about the narrative of hope surrounding literacy education in prison. While writing is no panacea for the brutal realities of the carceral state, for those living within the prison walls these statements provide evidence that writing can pro-vide significant personal transformation, as students revise their sense of themselves through a reconsideration of their histories, their current circumstances, and their futures.

China, serving a life sentence, thinks a great deal about his immi-grant family and the struggles of adjustment that contributed to some of the choices he made:

I write because I don't have a choice. Who else is going to be my voice, tell my story, and show my pain? Who will explain the failures of my generation? Who will teach them what I have learned? Who will inspire? You can say that after two decades of confinement, I have discovered many things about myself, those around me, and the world I wish to be a part of. I want to write about the people who feel deprived, displaced, and alienated. I want to write for those that feel like they don't belong, as if they are outside the mainstream culture. I want to write about the immigrants, refugees, and gangsters; those kids out on the corner curb serving crack rocks. I want to write for those who struggle with language barriers and feel trapped in an alien world. I want to explore the complexity of urban life, the unique communities and sub-communities that combine to make our society. I want to tell stories about families with missing parents whether it is because of the war, separations, divorce, or simply because they are consumed with work or their own miseries. I also would like to show how damaging the process of assimilation is, culture shock and the violence of identity formation are real. It is cold, cruel, and heartbreakingly uncompromising.

Johnny, another "lifer," thinks less about systems of oppression and more about sharing his own emotions:

I became a writer to convey my heartfelt emotions and understand why I hunger for love and what causes the irreparable scars on my battered heart. Through writing, I will learn and discern the true nature why I desire bitter and sweet sensations. Writing is an essential method to vent and expose my experiences to the world as I hope to unfetter someone's mind, spirit and give them an identity, as I did for myself.

Disclosing my wounds from love on paper or through songs takes courage because it is always difficult to relive suffered pasts. I hope to encourage and inspire people to utter their own unwanted pains and liberate the chains that encumbered them. I believe writing can heal the deepest gashes and restore a fragmented soul. My words are all I have and just knowing someone reads it makes me feel alive.

Lue wants to use writing not only to record his own personhood but also to acknowledge the lives of others. Writing, he says, is what will help others take him seriously. It also has helped him take himself seriously:

> The people that I am writing about are either here or maybe no longer around. I want people to know what these individuals have or had accomplished in their lives, who they are, the life that they lived, and what they had left behind. When I write, a poem, a short story, or a novel, I want my writing to grab my audience to the point where when they read or hear one of my writings, when they close their eyes that they can see through the eyes of the individual that I am writing about. I want my readers to experience everything: the things that the person that I am writing about have had went through, not only the goods but the bad as well. I want my writing to one day define who I am. That I take life seriously and I want everyone to have the same opportunity as I did and be able to share their life story to everyone else.

Chris takes on his status of incarceration directly in his writer's statement and struggles for self-worth in the belly of the carceral state:

> I write to vent my frustrations in a confrontational ploy to address the absurdity of locking us in cages like animals so that we will behave like people again. I find writing to be a practical means of liberation that calls for hard work and dedication, passing a simple task of enduring an oppressive setting. I see writing as a way to remain available amongst a disenfranchised population. There is a constant audit within my soul as I struggle to appraise my worth, examining my place in this society and what brought me here.
>
> I aspire to show people that we as felons are more than our greatest mistakes. There are people incarcerated that have spent years redefining their character and are no longer threats to society. We

represent the group with the highest potential to decrease recidivism rates by reaching out to struggling youth or peers that can relate to our past. Worth is abundant here; if it be used to help or heal in some way, to create that avenue is a prime goal. As my eyes adjust to the dark circumstance engulfing me, I intend to grab hold of my reader and transfix them with my perspective. Some may relate while others are enlightened; nonetheless, I hope to strike a curious spark to know more about me and the place trying to kill me.

LaVon, arrested on the steps of his high school, incarcerated as a juvenile, and in his 20th year of a life sentence, views writing as a kind of mentorship and therefore views himself as a kind of mentor:

> I write in hope of reaching some young men and women and help them to see that there are options in life that we often overlook. As a certified juvenile myself, I believe that I am obligated to try to reach these youth. That in reaching only some of them with my writing now matters. I want my legacy or imprint on this world to be large yet small. Large enough that my actions and words affect enough people that they can make a change. Although some seek a wave I only need a ripple. I believe that there are many layers to each of us. I'm just trying to share a sliver of each with every piece of literature that I write.

Ray, who has dealt with the demons of his childhood, finds writing to be a way to heal and to redefine himself:

> I write because it has become my passion, and my true first love. A place where I can bare my mind, heart, and soul to that child who think they are alone in this world. Who've witnessed abuse, drug and alcoholism, or gang violence and feel helpless. So I write for that child still trapped in me. I write to break all stereotypes about us as inmates. That we are just doing time, or a bunch of manipulating animals. I write to express our struggle, triumphs, and acts of humanity. To let people see we are fathers, brothers, uncles, cousins, and grandfathers. That a lot of us are working to better ourselves and

each other. I use writing to reach back into the communities I help destroy, and hopefully change at least one young man's life.

I write to challenge myself to grow as a man; and human being. I write so I never again have to hide from my problems, but face them head on. I write because the pen slows down my racing thought and anxiety. Once I reread what I've written, I'm forced to acknowledge my distorted thinking.

I write to escape prisons boundaries, and limitations. I write to release what helps confines me. My anger, fear, anxiety, and depression. I write to heal from betrayal, hurt, abandonment, and guilt. I write to uplift my self-esteem and find the astonishing qualities everyone else sees in me.

Isaac, new to writing and a short-timer, perhaps says it the most simply as he considers writing to be his vehicle for self-direction and purpose:

My written words today steer me on the path I go. I am writing to prove that I know I am about something.

These writers' statements, and the processes of writing that they record, offer evidence of a metacognitive awareness on the part of the incarcerated writers, that the educational enterprise of literate behavior changed their sense of themselves and to differing degrees the sense that others had of them. Individually, each is a tile, a token of how literacy can transform a life, revise a self. Together, they form a mosaic that, while it may be fairly viewed with skepticism and doubt, holds true accomplishment and promise for the writers, both individually and as a collective.

Conclusion

After the reading of the creative writing class, which I described at the beginning of the chapter, some of the lifers were transferred from the high-security prison to medium-security: Ross and China. Ostensibly, they were eligible for the move after serving 25 years. Yet I couldn't help but wonder if the commissioner's attendance at that reading had some effect on the decisions he made about whom to transfer. His words again rang in my ear, as I learned about each transfer:

"I see sons, fathers, husbands, all in those words, and I can see how you have changed. That event that got you in here, it is in your past. It should be retreating into the rearview mirror. It is not who you are, and it does not define you. This is who you are. Your words define you."

Reading their words not only transformed their sense of themselves, but it also transformed the commissioner's sense of them. And his sense of them transformed the nature, the fabric, the texture, and in some cases, even the eventual length of their incarceration.

Knowledge Is Truly Food For Our Souls

Tonight was the first night of a new class, one that I am teaching with John Schmit, an English professor at Augsburg College. It's a sociolinguistics class called Language and Power. On this first night it all came flooding back why teaching here seems so important, why it is both exhilarating and devastating, why I eagerly spend my sabbatical in this grim and gritty place.

In the enthusiastic flush of the classroom, it is easy to forget that the men spend much of their time in a dank 6 by 9 cell. Once in the classroom, though, the grimness recedes and the classroom becomes remarkably like most class-rooms in many surprising ways. As the men enter the classroom, I am thrilled to see that eight of the twenty-four are students from previous classes. We greet each as warmly as this frigid and unforgiving place will allow. A firm handshake with smiles is what we all seem to settle on. Still, when they say, "Welcome back. Good to see you again," I hesitate as I think of what to say in return that is neither insincere nor insensitive. Because here the queries "How are you? How have you been?" even "What's up?" all seem fraught in a place that last week led one of their fellow prisoners to suicide . . . in his cell.

We discuss the syllabus and the basic premises of language and power, the axis around which the course spins. In our first linguistic exercise, we ask them to write down their most and least favorite words. We giggle when one student has to explain that "good looking" means thanks, not you're, well, good looking. John laughs at his own disappointment, having been the hypotheti-cal recipient of this compliment. In fact, the men explain, it is short for "good looking out," meaning "thanks for having my back."

There are sympathetic nods when LaVon explains that his least favorite word is "when" because he doesn't have an answer when his daughter asks when will he come home (we all know the answer: he's not coming home). We all take in a sharp breath when both "nigger" and "white boy" are offered, from opposite sides of the room, as least favorite words. The tension is palpable, and we all keenly feel the possibilities for an eruption. This is both the safest and the most dangerous classroom I've ever stepped foot in.

At the end of class we pass out cards and we ask them to feel free to write down anything they'd like to say. We receive two cards from two of our returning students. Here's what they wrote:

> I just want to say it's great to have the both of you back!

B.'s note

> Thank you dearly for coming back! Nothing is more liberating (to me) than access to knowledge.
> Knowledge is truly food for our souls.

Eli's note

These hastily scrawled sentiments remind me of why I am here: these learners are as hungry and as sincere as any I have ever had the privilege to teach. And they have souls that need to be nourished.

CHAPTER SIX

Writing in the Dark
PROFILES OF INCARCERATED LEARNERS

DEHUMANIZATION IS ONE of the required tactics of "successful" incarceration. Individuals are reduced to virtually nameless prisoners known and directly addressed by their Offender Identification Numbers (OIDs). Individual needs, characteristics, and histories are blurred into a collective identity of a cellblock of "offenders." In volunteer training we are told that it is critically important not to distinguish any individual "offender" through differentiated treatment, since it might cause resentment and hostility among prisoners and misperceptions about volunteers' intent, motivation, or emotional investment. Movement from cellblock to cafeteria, cafeteria to work, work to classroom, occurs en masse. Even getting medication is accomplished in a group event called "pill run," which unceremoniously interrupts gatherings, meetings, even classes. Attending to or even acknowledging the contours of individuality can be seen as a security threat. It is easier to cage someone when you don't think of them as human.

The general public, too, tends to think of "the incarcerated" as a mass noun. We know little of the individual stories that comprise the master narrative of mass incarceration. We generalize who the incarcerated might be; it would be almost unbearable to conjure the faces and voices of those who in many ways are not very different from us. We make assumptions about their family background, their educational attainment or lack thereof, their psychological profiles, their moral compass or code, their ethnicity, and their social class.

While it is indeed regrettably true, as Michelle Alexander (2010) and others have demonstrated, that incarceration affects the poor and communities of color in disproportionate numbers, there is a surprisingly wide diversity in the prison population. In the prison where I teach, some of the incarcerated are white (40%), some have high school diplomas or GEDs (81%), some come from outside the major metro area (38%), and some are from a different state (2%). Some are younger than twenty (2%) and some are older than sixty-five (2%) (Department of Corrections, 2018). They defy generalization. Their complex and varied paths to incarceration challenge our simplistic notion of who lives behind bars and why. Their stories are as varied and textured as those who live on the outside, and their identities are more faceted than the monochromatic prison blues or oranges they wear. In the following pages, you will meet a middle-class white man, an African American incarcerated at eighteen for life, a Hmong writer and artist, and a Latinx college student. For each of them, education in general and literacy education in particular have played critical roles in their lives behind bars.

Chris

Chris's angelic looks disguise the hardship he has experienced, both in and out of prison. He is astonishingly handsome, with the looks of a Latino telenovela star. His clear brown skin is beginning to be covered with ever-growing tattoos, but his face is still babyish and innocent. He generally has a quiet and understated demeanor, one that belies his penchant for aggressive leadership and his sometimes-dark moods. Like many of the incarcerated students with whom I have worked, Chris is a gifted visual artist as well as writer. This seeming coincidence of talent continues to confound me. Why are so many of the incarcerated so gifted at representing in both words and pictures the world they left behind?

Chris has been incarcerated for over ten years for participation in a gang-related drive-by in which he was not the shooter but an accomplice. Merely being a passenger in a car involved in a shooting is considered a felony in some states. Unlike many of the men with whom I work, he has an out date. When he is released, he will have spent more than half his life in prison.

Chris has devoted himself to the craft of writing. He has drawn inspiration from the example of Jimmy Santiago Baca, whom he considers to be a kind of patron saint. For Chris, Baca models both the salvation that writing can serve in prison as well as the possibility that prison writers can receive legitimate literary appreciation on the outside. Here is his writer's statement:

Writer's Statement

"And the day came when the risk to remain tight in a bud
Was more painful than the risk it took to blossom"
–Anais Nin

"We are healed of our suffering only by experiencing it to the full."
–Marcel Proust

Years ago, I resolved that I would not die in this place. The mind, body, and spirit are in constant flux in prison's toxic and unstable environments, a world suspended, dangling between punishment and self rehabilitation. After adjusting to the death of who I was in the world, I figured that prison will merely be a setting in which a substantial portion of my life will play out. However limited, I still have choices, opportunities, and influence.

My roots are in visual art. I wasn't a heavy reader and never tried to write creatively. A few friends wrote stories and recommended that I start journaling. I got involved in higher education and was introduced to creative writing formats through a trusted professor.

My poetry is a processed venting of emotion that I refine into something I can grasp. The nonfiction pieces I write through a lens of advocacy, designed to initiate an alternative regard to the societal assumptions that construct my surroundings. The fiction and personal memoir I construct to make sense of topics such as forgiveness, redemption, and unrequited love; such that mirror my efforts in visual art.

I write to vent my frustrations in a confrontational ploy to address the absurdity of locking us in cages like animals so that we will behave like people again. I find writing to be a practical means of liberation that calls for hard work and dedication, passing a simple task of enduring an oppressive setting. I see writing as a way to remain available amongst a disenfranchised population. There is a constant audit within my soul as I struggle to appraise my worth, examining my place in this society and what brought me here. I am working on bridging my writing and visual art so that they do not simply replicate a message but complement each other in a way that expands the scope of meaning past a point they express as individuals.

I am currently developing a series of works exploring the things that get us through the vapid years of waiting. Places like the visiting room and all of the different interests and ideals it represents. Simple things like the power of writing paper and envelopes covering the arid deserts that keep people from saying the things they feel. And the importance of photographs, of cherished moments with people lost or of simpler times; or pictures of celebrities or places that represent an unknown future of possibility.

I aspire to show people that we as felons are more than our greatest mistakes. There are people incarcerated that have spent years redefining their character and are no longer threats to society. We represent the group with the highest potential to decrease recidivism rates by reaching out to struggling youth or peers that can relate to our past. Worth is abundant here; if it be used to help or heal in some way, to create that avenue is a prime goal. As my eyes adjust to the dark circumstance engulfing me, I intend to grab hold of my reader and transfix them with my perspective. Some may relate while others are enlightened; nonetheless, I hope to strike a curious spark to know more about me and the place trying to kill me.

▪ ▪ ▪

With a fellow prisoner, Chris founded the writers' collective at the prison, which serves as an example of the community of practice discussed earlier. This collective has garnered increasing power and autonomy. The collective meets regularly to support the writing of the prisoners, helping accomplished writers hone their craft and find publishing venues and encouraging novice writers to join their ranks. The collective sponsors forums on articles about writing and readings that include both inside and outside writers.

In partnership with the nonprofit organization that offers writing classes in other facilities, the writers' collective helps choose class offerings and even, with the assistance of the education director, vets other prisoners for classes. These prisoners serve as tutors in those classes, which range from playwriting and poetry to creative nonfiction. Some have even begun teaching introductory writing classes on their own. It is gratifying to watch these men evolve over time from tentative students to confident teachers.

Chris's role in the writers' collective seemed to change the power dynamic between him and Department of Corrections personnel. For example, at one meeting with a couple of teachers from the outside and the education director, Chris was present as a co-participant. At a writers' forum, which focused on an essay by a contemporary writer, Chris became the de facto leader and facilitator even though that role was supposed to be shared with a teacher/writer from the outside.

Chris was deeply invested in the community of practice that the collective became. It offered him power and authority but also sometimes caused blurred lines between him and corrections personnel as well as occasional resentment with fellow prisoners. Still, Chris's participation in the writers' collective as well as his consistent efforts as a writer became the most salient part of his self-narrative.

Chris uses writing to explore his childhood, remembering, for example, in a piece called "Smurphs on the Wall," visiting his father as a child in the very prison in which he is now incarcerated. He uses writing to sort out and express his emotions. He writes:

> So much of doing prison time is anger and frustration. Simply put, oppression makes you angry. Writing taught me how to organize my emotions in a relatable manner. Writing teaches me how to be a better listener as well. It helps me develop empathy in thinking about characterization and analyzing how my work relates to a general human condition. I see people in a more objective light. Emotions are universal. In communication I am seeking to bond with another person. How can I best convey my thoughts in order to be the most authentic I can be?

. . .

Chris also uses writing to address romantic loves, sometimes real and sometimes imagined. A multigenre writer, he writes essays, creative nonfiction, and poetry, and recently had a poem accepted by a prominent literary magazine.

Chris is perhaps at his best, although he might disagree, when he expresses, in essay form, his experience of incarceration. Here is an excerpt from an essay entitled "A Certain Kind":

> It's the sounds that lull you: the bells as a training device for animals, jingling of keys, an ever presence of authority, a constant murmur of voices until suddenly it stops. I grab the panel of steel bars and begin to close my own door, sliding on a track with the momentum of a roller coaster before the slam echoes in my core. These are the sounds that sink to silence leading you to believe this is an option you chose. I didn't have to fight anyone today, I probably won't fight tomorrow—but tonight, like every night, I'll fight the idea that I belong here, in this cage.
>
> I think of all the men around me, with experience lying dormant under the soot of poor decisions. I know not many are scribbling in notebooks. I understand that when everything you've built is lost to a moment of impulse it is dangerous to believe that anything you craft is safe from your fire. It is a hard sell to convince a guy to start over and build on the shifty prison sands of an hourglass continually shaken. It's natural to focus on distraction and want to simply endure a prison sentence. It's sad to think that most of these stories, the ones truly worth telling, will perish in the dignity found in forgetting. Destruction begets destruction and prison kills your spirit; but creativity can resuscitate the soul. Unfortunately writing is not for everyone.
>
> We are individualistic, selfish and starving for scraps of attention the caged crave. The nature of prison encapsulates you at your lowest hour and threatens to never let you go.
>
> We are responsible for atrocious acts, and this is no small thing to consider. It's protocol for people to want to take us for who we are today and shun the past moral barriers we have breached but to deny these realities is to live in denial of the deepest darkest impulses that linger at the primal bedrock of the human condition.

The problem lies in our inability to endure such contradicting emotions while holding people accountable. What do we do when a human being strays from the boundaries we set for humankind, and how do we bring them back into the fold of humanity—once we have caged them? One way is writing.

In writing we find the opportunity to develop a bond with society through audience. It's not simply about being heard, but about acknowledging the responsibility of listening. Through critiques, dissecting works and public readings we are taught how to pay attention to the world around us. In doing this, we cannot help but discover the thread that binds us all together in this human condition.

Writing is the epitome of self-rehabilitation. There are no certificates for a base file, no credits for a degree to show at the end of an investment. A simple work represents years of sweat and tears and might be submitted for rejection time and time again. But the writer emerges from that work with a new understanding.

This is the creative life—what Oscar Wilde called the long lovely suicide. If prison is a trapdoor at rock bottom, then writing is the mortar in between the bricks you must pry in order to dig your way out.

The truth of the matter is that writing is hard. It takes a certain kind of crazed obsession no matter what your environment. *If everyone has a story to tell, why aren't some ever told?* How many of us have compromised the craft for family or friends, to raise children or teach others?

Writing requires a balance of living a life worth writing about and doing the work. In the process you are changed, and the moment of epiphany comes when you begin to read your *life* as a writer. Everything around you becomes part of the craft. You see the plot in the narratives unfolding in real time. You can realize relationships are complex characters making the decisions you may or may not agree with. People couldn't script some of the shit you go through, so you mold it as a lesson to be learned.

It takes a certain kind of will to begin to pick up shattered pieces of a life laid before us. It takes a certain kind of courage to mourn what was broken and confront the value of that which was lost by our hand. It takes a certain kind of creativity to craft those broken shards, through audacity and hope, into something that pays respect to the past yet bears a responsibility to a future. And it takes a certain kind of benevolence to invest in the fallen—a complex compassion that can forgive without forgetting, that believes that moving on doesn't absolve accountability.

In my cramped cell, where I eat, work, and sleep mere feet from a toilet, I sit and ponder how to use this fleeting moment—what to say to you lightning bugs who have wandered into our glass jars. Through continued support convicts can come home better people; but the formula is flawed. Enduring a retributive prison sentence does little to honor our victims. It's in taking hold of our story that we can still turn it around for a greater good. Only in finding a form of success can we get to a point where we can help others. We must combat that insurmountable debt—a debt we owe not to society, but to humanity.

Don't wait until we are released to invest in us. Everyone needs to be heard in order to know the value of their voice. The dignity of the damned must be redeemed. Go tell your friends, family, co-workers, politicians, anyone who will listen that we exist—for better or worse. And we will continue to grow and refine our voice until it is amplified to the explosive degree that blows a hole in the wall. Not for us to escape, but for society to see inside and explore ideas of justice in a place we are all taught to fear and dismiss.

■ ■ ■

Here is one of Chris's poems:

THAT PICTURE ON THE WALL
Tiny torn rolled tabs of masking tape
chip through layers of decades old paint,
fracturing the concrete wall of a cell,
carving out a window sill that frames her
through a simple photo hanging on the wall.

Rays radiate from her gaze, speaking through
Cherry wood irises, chestnut varnished shine,
table tops reflecting ivory place sets of fine china
for the dinner of a happy home never being.
The whites of her eye scream, running from the shadowy
recesses of mascara, hiding the pain of elephant bones.

> I've been down those corridors,
> back alleys cold and wet,
> something stank, always dripping
> in puddles with cig butts and needles.
> Nights layered in musky clothes,
> under soiled blankets that mumble
> the lies of a childhood, and whisper
> the future that we dream to forget.

Her high cheekbone hills lined with rosy reds
soft and sincere, below masks of make-up
needing more than tears and backhands.
Her dimples pierced like the hands of Christ,
steel studs, tough guys too hard to be hard,
two thieves between the salvation of her lips
calling from a world of adults wanting to be kids
so that the kids had to be the adults.

> I grew up in those houses too,
> where parents die and fears
> are the dreams that come true.
> Red wrappers of Nut Roll candy bars
> and green stripes on Kool 100's packs
> became our religion, crossing oo's
> like the rings of magicians as miracles.

Her vibrant ink rides the highway curves
of glorious valleys and mountaintops without
breaks or seatbelts; revving my heartbeat in Cali sun.

Bruised by a thousand needle pokes marching,
telling the tales of a resilient revolution. Her beauty
scars speak an earned language; an honored anguish,
unparalleled to the emotional war
of a tortured soul grown strong.

> I got some of my ink
> thinking of her and I
> wonder if she'll ever
> know she is worth it.
> Even if not.
> She's a spit shined badge,
> Recalling a blood oath with
> God and Devil within.

She sees me;
can finish my sentences and won't hesitate to call 'bullshit.'
She gets where I've been & believes in where I'm going.
She's never late, doesn't lie unless I ask her to; never misses calls or blows off mail.

> It doesn't matter
> that I've never met her,
> or felt neck hairs
> stand at her touch.
> So what, I couldn't
> be the one to wipe tears
> with my thumbs or lips.

She's what pleads to hold the beast at bay in the hollow of my cave when
criminal clichés are all I see. She's what's on the back of my eyelids keeping
tears from turning into toxins; urging me not to give-up, whispering the flutter
of butterfly wings tracing tracks dancing in sparks of love. She is faith, telling
me I am worth the fight to be a better man as I live out days from expendable
binds clutching the ideals of her through bleeding fists.

. . .

Chris articulates his goal for writing this way:

> My goal is to normalize inmates, to build a bridge and paint a human picture on incarceration. Too often people see prisons as completely foreign places with animal-like beings that are unrelatable. I want to show people that there are people just like them. I'll get out one day. Then publishing avenues will open up to me and I'll use them to be a voice for the disenfranchised.

• • •

For the most part, Chris's experience with the liberal arts has been positive and transformative. However, like other astute observers of education in prison, Chris realizes its limits. He writes:

Chris's rendering of "Words No Bars Can Hold"

There is no doubt that my educational experiences have made me a better person, but there is a negative side as well. In the face of meeting a rehabilitative goal, I hit a glass ceiling. There is a shelf life where education/betterment begins to be mocked by limitation and lack of opportunities. I know I could have been more, done more with my life had I not ignored my potential in the first place. And I know it's the only hand worth playing right now within the circumstances I find myself in. But what is the point to it all if I'm not able to use it for the good of others?

. . .

Fong

Fong belongs to a population that is increasingly found in Midwest prisons: the Hmong. As one of the most recent waves of refugees, fleeing from Laos and Cambodia and resettling in the United States, the Hmong have had many challenges adjusting to life in their adopted homeland. Language and cultural barriers have made economic and generational stability elusive, and though there have been some significant strides and success, there is still endemic poverty, violence, and gang structure in some quarters of the community (Lee, 2001). Adjustment to life in the United States for the Hmong is varied both generationally and by gender. Once one of my Hmong college students lamented to me, "Hmong women go to college, but too many of our men go to prison" (Lo, 2017).

Like many of his counterparts, Fong and his family had a difficult time in their adopted homeland. He describes his childhood in the following way:

As far as my childhood goes, I was raised in a strict traditional family where hierarchy plays a major role. Affection was never expressed. When expressing affection does happen, it comes through criticism. Strict parents with high expectation for their children to be good sons and daughters, I often got yelled at and punished for siblings' wrongs as well as my own. Their strictness hindered my understanding of the world. This led me to act up to justify the punishments from father.

Both of my parents have no educational background. We came to United States as refugee of war. In U.S. my father was ruled illiterate. He was denied a driver license—never got a driver license to this day. Never will.

In my household, there are a total of 12 people living under one roof: eight children, father, mother, an uncle and grandmother. Uncle and grandmother have no educational background either. Agrarian people.

My parents have ten children all together but the two oldest boys died when they were kids in Laos. That leaves eight of us. Birth order: girl, boy, boy, boy, girl, boy, boy, and girl. I am the sixth child of the eight.

The Detroit school was no help either. The lack of security at school, inadequate textbooks, teachers who care, counselors, ESL programs (English Second Language), opened the door for me to start skipping school with older cousins and friends. I did no school sports. I started smoking and drinking at the age of nine. By 14, drinking, smoking, skipping school, fighting, breaking girls' hearts, gambling, traveling from state to state, stealing cars, clothes, shoes, foods, bikes you name it, all these things became normal, daily activities. As well as combating other races because of racial tension. And other Asians for the supremacy of one's gang.

• • •

Although he managed not to get into serious trouble during his adolescence, adulthood heralded more difficulty as fractures in friendship groups became serious and the stuff of sometimes deadly scuffles. In his late twenties, Fong was caught up in an altercation that left another Hmong man dead. He was found guilty of aiding and abetting a murder and is in his 14th year of a 25-year sentence.

Like Chris, Fong is a gifted visual artist and is enlisted by others whenever a thank-you note or special painting needs to be created. His artist's palate is in stark contrast to the grays, blacks, and beiges that surround him in prison. He favors soft pastels—greens, pinks, yellows, and blues—and paints bucolic images of cranes and oceans. He laughs easily and is well-liked by his fellow prisoners. His eagerness to please and overall cooperative spirit have endeared him to his teachers and to corrections personnel.

On the outside, Fong barely managed to finish high school and was not particularly interested in higher education. Unlike Chris, Fong came to writing late and reluctantly. In the very first writing class he took with me, he struggled. He wasn't able to complete any writing assignments and said he was experiencing serious writers' block, even though, he said, he "really wasn't a writer yet" and didn't know if he qualified for a writer's dilemma.

I asked Fong, who spends his "free" time teaching other Hmong prisoners their mother tongue, what language he dreamed in. He said he dreams in Hmong. "Try writing in Hmong first," I told him, "and then you can translate it into English once you have your ideas and images on paper." This technique worked for him and opened a floodgate of creative writing. Here was his first effort:

SEVERAL QUESTIONS

Hmoob os Hmoob—
what have we become? Did
we forget to wash our eyes
this morning? Have we forgotten
the burden our ancestors carried
so we could be free? Should we
curse the venerated
shamans who gave us identity?
Have we lose our identity as
those who *coj xauv tshuab qeej*
tshuab ncas, ntaus nruas ua neeb
ua yaig? And *ntaus kuam hu plig*
khi tes? If we have, are we still
Hmoob then? What about how we
broke culture norms? And accept
taboos such as copulation between
lis and lis? yaj thiab yaj? tub thaib tub? Ntxchais and ntxchais?
Should we eat bread? Cheese? Say
no to rice & chili peppers—would
that make us American then?
Should we let our brothers
& sisters rot in American prisons?
& let them be nothing more than
a mistake? Should we erase them

from society? *Hmoob*—when
did we become selfish? Why do we
wait until we lay in our graves
to search for salvation? How I love
for you to know that *Lis Foom*
wrote this poem? And not
inmate-two one seven eight
zero five?
what have we become?
Hmoob os Hmoob—

. . .

Soon after his first creative writing class, Fong became a board member of the writers' collective and an integral member of the writing community. He has, after fits and starts, newly committed himself to pursuing higher education and has improved his attendance, which was always haphazardly enthusiastic yet sometimes erratic. He still struggles with the gathering darkness that seems to regularly settle on the horizon of the incarcerated and has fits of inadequacy and self-doubt. But writing has given him a way to affirm his Hmong identity and, at the same time, offer an alternative reality to the one defined by his Offender Identification Number and his prison blues. Here is one of his latest poems:

WHAT I HAVE BEEN DOING
Not a vast ocean.
Not a deep lake.
I crawl the cracked asphalt
Of a Midwest penitentiary
       Stillwater
collecting salt water.
Fold it—tuck it
inside an envelope,
mail it to a world
that does not
write
me
back.

. . .

LaVon

LaVon has become a man in prison. Arrested before he was eighteen on the steps of his city high school for a gang-related gunfight, LaVon has a sentence of more than two lifetimes. He recently cut off his waist-length dreadlocks and shaved his head. When I asked him what prompted him to get rid of his signature hair, he said it was his 20th year in prison and his fortieth birthday. "I thought I should mark it in some way," he said. "Happy birthday to me."

LaVon is a lifer. The warden once told me that lifers are the stability of the prison, the solid citizens of the carceral city. They somehow become habituated to their incarcerated lives and settle in. They work, they study, they paint, they pray. They alternate between working feverishly on their appeals and studying the law, and becoming resigned to this place that, as one of them told me, they'll "leave in a pine box." They become members of a complex society with rules and hierarchies of its own. Long bids like LaVon's command respect. There is a hierarchy of crimes as well, with such things as child molestation on the very bottom.

In addition to his 114-year sentence, LaVon brings his street credibility into the prison. He has an air of quiet authority about him. I later came to realize that that authority bears resonance to the authority he had on the streets so long ago. He is the kingpin, the chief, the godfather, as he is colloquially known. Yet none of his considerable gravitas is animated as swagger. He is serious and soft-spoken, although he will occasionally burst out in song as he recites his poetry, a combination of spoken word and Whitmanesque free verse.

LaVon was in the first class I taught more than a decade ago and has been in every one since. He approaches learning with such seriousness of purpose, with such reverence, that he alone can make the classroom seem holy. In our first class, an Introduction to Literature course, he wrote an original poem to complement every academic essay. He finished his GED in prison and has been pursuing education ever since. He doesn't care about earning a degree—his credits are scattered haphazardly across a variety of online institutions and disciplines. He wants to *learn* things, he once told me, not *earn* things.

Unlike most of the other writers with whom I have worked, LaVon has no interest in publishing his writing or sharing it with a larger audience. While he is a frequent and enthusiastic participant in our public readings, he writes primarily for himself, as he states in his writer's statement:

Writer's Statement

Quote by Langston Hughes

"What is poetry?" Langston Hughes asked.
Then answered, "It is the human soul entire,
squeezed like a lemon or lime, drop by drop,
into atomic words."

I write because it is my therapy, a way for me to tell my story and deal with my life experiences in a healthy fashion. I write in hope of reaching some young men and women and help them to see that there are options in life that we often overlook. As a certified juvenile myself, I believe that I am obligated to try to reach these youth. That in reaching only some of them with my writing now matters.

I am what I call a reflective writer. I write about my life experiences; how my environment and or culture and the events within it affect me. I write about my reflections on social events in the world and the coverage of certain events or the lack of and why they matter so much to me. Currently I am working on five books; my first attempt at a fantasy novel, which I believe is coming along pretty good. The second book is the first installment of a trilogy of urban fiction. The third is a fictional drama that I'm experimenting with. The last two are collections of poetry plus a chapbook.

I've lost a lot of close people in my life so find myself writing a lot of odes and elegies. But I've played with a lot with poetic writing styles like, pantoums, sestinas and of course free verse. I'm a large fan of spoken word and slam poetry and love to perform myself.

I try to write stylistically so that it reads as it sounds when performed. I want my legacy or imprint on this world to be large yet small. Large enough that my actions and words affect enough people that they can make a change. Although some seek a wave, I only need a ripple. I believe that there are many layers to each of us. I'm just trying to share a sliver of each with every piece of literature that I write.

• • •

LaVon views writing as a vehicle of self-improvement, of bettering himself, of trying to become the man he hopes he can someday be. He believes in transformation, even if it will only take place within the walls of the prison. His commitment to self-improvement is unshakable, and as with his writing, he is the only audience that matters. He also sees it as a way to heal and to come to terms with the life he is living behind bars. With no discernable way out, LaVon creates a community in prison. In many ways it has become his city, his neighborhood, his world.

Yet he is fiercely aware of things on the outside. He studies politics and sociology. He was deeply moved by the election of Barack Obama and unsettled by what he perceives to be the rise of racism since the election of Donald Trump. He is taken with the Black Lives Matter movement, and some of his poetry is searingly political. For example, he wrote this poem in response to the spate of slayings of African American men by police:

BLACK LIVES DON'T MATTER
Black lives don't matter!
Not since the slave trade gathered
among the western shores of Africa
and they all scattered.

Not since sea salt
cauterized wounds, or soap
boxes sat in show case
rooms for auction.

Since then, it's been
whips and chains, nooses
and K-9's,
plus sprayed nines
and cane dimes.

There are hate crimes
plus engraved signs
encased within cement lines,
that cements lines
which are bought
with black lives.

I said,
there are hate crimes plus engraved signs
encased within cement lines,
that cement lines which are bought
with black lives.

While you march for attention
end up in local detention;
they often fail to mention
before every grand jury decision,
The facts were based on dissention.

Like their opinion of a symbol of hate
"But the flags true intention . . ."

Justice wasn't born blind.
She turns a blind eye
as tipped scales overcrowd brick cells,
that happen to be full of black males.

Like me
so I guess I failed

A burden no cross could weigh.
But my shoulders cave
like the last brick of the largest pyramid
carried by one slave.

I'm sorry,
but there is no white hand
that can lift us up
out of the blood sweat and tears
we've cried, shed and smeared.

There is no justice to be found
within the mouths of those
who whisper,
"Yeah, he was gunned down, but, but, but . . ."

What should I expect,
as rally cries
drown out mother's cries
as their sons die
from led poisoning
due to crossed barred
nooses around their necks?

If 137 shots in Ohio isn't premeditation
how can only 2,
after a 3 month investigation?

Or a legal strangulation,
being shot while ordered
to retrieve license and registration.
Or being a child in a park
seeking recreation.

Police chief apologies
only compound the frustration
of another father burying his son
realizing that his heir,
has arrived at another destination.

Six degrees of separation
comes back to segregation
as well as mass incarceration
until we find a resolution
to the cultural self-pollution
believing we can only go far
as a Rap star or a Trap star.

We'll only live in a world seen
from the perspective,
of a blind eye!

Now I can raise my fist
but the intent will be missed
unlike adding emphasis
to the line, "Stop Resist
-ing!"

Why persist
in denial of this:
I exist!
Not to be a mockery of
In the name of justice.

Simply that my life matters
As much or more than just this,
187406

· · ·

In many ways LaVon exemplifies what can only be described as the purity of literary pursuit in prison. Literacy is not a means to any kind of instrumental end—not vocational, not educational in the traditional sense of attaining degrees through postsecondary education. LaVon won't be up for parole (there is really no such thing in our state) for eventual release or for commutation. LaVon writes to heal himself, to map the contours of his interior landscape and in doing so to rechart it. He writes:

> Writing has been my key to freedom. With the kind of time that I am facing it is easy to become bogged down with the idea that I have nothing left to offer life or that life has nothing left to offer me. Yet through writing I am able to live, I am able to give and receive a sense of peace that I would not be able to have found nowhere else behind these walls. Writing has become everything for me, it literally has saved me. When I found out how to express myself through a pen I knew from that point forward life would be worth living. I have purpose now.

. . .

In long bids like LaVon's, even family members might cease to visit. LaVon thinks often about the family he left behind. Although incarcerated as an adolescent, he was already a father when he went to prison. He recently wrote the following ode to a long-lost daughter:

JASMINE
1
As the wind blows
your exhale captures
a song's rhythm.

I remember that song
like a lover's first
your many firsts I missed.
But I envision them in dreams.

Of awakening to your cry
only to calm your worry.
As you suckle on my finger,
one of your favorite things.

How your soft, delicate hands
become strong
as I try to remove my finger
Smiling as you fill my nose

and pamper with your smell.
Bringing tears to my eyes
as I awaken from that fading smile
to a guard's frown.

2
Oh Jazzy.
How I wish to see you
in that peach flowered dress,
hear those Osh Kosh sandals
running past.

Laugh when,
momma gets frustrated
wiping your sticky hands
while I steadily feed you
chocolate.

Last night I didn't dream
about how you always respond
to the sound of my voice
no matter what you're doing.

You would be 17 yrs. old now.
How the time has passed.
Jasmine,
do you still laugh?

As the sun lit rays
peek through a cloud
are you looking down?

Jasmine.
My soul hasn't been whole
since the day God
took you away.

But when I dream
he allows me to see you,
only in heaven's light.

3
And your star-lit eyes
shine brighter than
your sun-kissed skin,
your drool soaked grin.

And you're beautiful,
so beautiful.

I miss you Jasmine.

• • •

Zeke

White middle-class families in the United States have the luxury of
not expecting their sons or daughters to go to prison. To be sure, the
odds are against it. Reports on the current state of incarceration in the
United States report that people of color are incarcerated at a significantly higher rate than whites. For example, the Prison Policy Initiative
from the Bureau of Justice statistics estimates that the rate of incarceration per 100,000 is 380 for whites and 2207 for blacks (Wagner,
2012). Zeke grew up as the adored only child in a middle-class family.
His home life was relatively stable, and he didn't lack for any material
needs. Yet, as Abraham Maslow reminds us, food, shelter, and safety
are merely basic needs and don't guarantee self-actualization or, in
other words, a state of satisfied well-being (Maslow, 1943). Zeke's basic
needs were always met; his parents saw to that, but their love and care
weren't enough to keep him out of prison.

Although he is one of the most intellectually gifted students I have ever taught, anywhere, Zeke barely graduated from high school. High school completely bored him and he began to skip classes and spend more time on the streets, falling in with a tough, streetwise crowd. Depression also took hold or, as Zeke himself explains, he fell in love with the grays. That depression remained undiagnosed and untreated until his first stint in jail.

A series of unsuccessful jobs, recurring depressive episodes, broken relationships, and shady associates in early adulthood led him to being in the wrong place at the wrong time. A robbery gone bad, an innocent life needlessly lost, and a fouled-up plea led him to a sentence of 25 years. He has been in prison for 20 of those years. In that time, Zeke's mother, father, and grandmother have all died, and with his parents' early untimely and unexpected deaths, his isolation has made even the harsh reality of incarceration more difficult. He has no family to visit him, and many of his former friends have lost contact with him over time.

Education has been a central focus of Zeke's incarceration, even though he has had many distractions and impediments in his pursuit of education. He has earned an AA degree and is working his way through a bachelor's degree. He has learned the value of reading:

> There were books I read that influenced my sensibilities. *Steppenwolf* appealed to some of my very dark experiences with loneliness and isolation and depression. Some books I read illuminated associations I had with injustice and individuals' confrontation with power, and some just taught me about the nuance of individual human lives. The books I read made me want to write things that touched people in the same ways.

• • •

Motivated by his reading as well as his desire to communicate his "experiences with the world," Zeke began to work seriously on his writing:

> Writing offered me a conduit to communicate my experiences with the world. It was not therapy but it could speak for me in ways nothing else could. It also offered me some evidence that I was still a feel-

ing and empathetic human being. When I was first able to publish, it offered a way for people I had lost contact with years before to reconnect. It was the way I could tell them where I had been. But as far as my break-me-down-to-my purpose reasons for writing: Writing was for me an act of defiance. I lived an entire life so deeply defined by roles hidden under varying levels of authority. It was the only way I could show that I hadn't been beaten by these people, even when I was so tired and worn down by being a prisoner. Also, writing for me was humbling, giving me space to confront all of the conflated parts of our being—ego and narcissism, pride exaggerated purpose. Through it, writing also became an act of endearment to my family, and to my city.

▪ ▪ ▪

Zeke has been writing prose and poetry since early in his incarceration. A multigenre, multitalented writer, he has won several PEN writing awards for poetry, short story, and memoir. He recently published a book-length memoir, one that was a finalist for a nonfiction book award. Becoming a published author held a particular salience for Zeke. He writes:

> There was for a while a transcendence from my incarceration; an idea that I had outperformed the strictures of this place, regardless of what the system or the nameless blob of power that governed over me expected of me. There is power in that feeling, and empowerment is what men in these places need most; the sense that they are capable human beings who can accomplish larger goals in their lives.

▪ ▪ ▪

This poem is exemplary of his well-honed craft:

THESE SONGS REMIND ME
These songs remind me
of rain clouds in my daylight,
When the rain used to swallow me.
Perfumed afternoons,

the faint specks of sunshine
on the windshield
of a cold and miserable
life

The darkened heart
that consumes men
with its separated incisors,
inside great-big gaping holes of silence
in the middle of the night,
where there are still plenty of hours
before my dawn.

And my pen bleeds
Just like me.
Just like me,
Cutting just deep enough
to leave a scar
to remember me,
because moments like these
melt in mercury.

And it was all so beautiful,
until I fell in love with the grays
and black of rainy afternoons,
running around outside
in the monsoon.

And the chords in the song
play my life
in soft pitch,
with hovering homonyms
of Dr. Pepper bottle memoirs
and gasoline mirages.

And it plays like the rain.
beating like crowded beats
in loud streets,
and the small drips
from a fragile ceiling.

Sleeping in paradoxical puddles,
trudging through tributaries
in the truth.
But I love the rain.

We were those snotty-nosed
wipe it on the front
of your coat kids
that sang
"We are the World"
and the "Greatest Love of All"
at public school presentations.
In front of
exhausted public school parents,
working 60-hour weeks
for somebody else's fortune.
That showed up
with ready-made smiles
and instant tears.

But the music doesn't stop
and the rain keeps playing
and their noses keep running
until the many-faced little monsters
fall in love with their cages.
Staring at the world
with bright eyes
in dim light,
that only see rainy nights.
But we love the rain!

We are the children
that used to be the future.
the dried brooks in a crook's eyes,
absorbed by that oblivious sponge
inside the ordinary inertia
of being human.
Dreams that live and die
in a wet abyss
with broken fingers
at the end of clenched fists.

This is the social tsunami
individuals
in strangled, strychnine
paradigms
playing their instruments
and singing songs
about the way we were,
                    and always will be.

                    ▪ ▪ ▪

And here is a poem that won second place in a PEN Prison Writing
contest:

PEOPLE I KNOW
The people I know
move and drift like smoke.
Who speak to the storms in their lives
and live in tornadoes
that come through, recklessly taking
        and rearranging things
            with all the indiscriminate power
                of God's hands on the lives
                    of his worshippers.

The people I know
  raise babies that aren't theirs,
  pulled from the rubble
      too scared to cry.
The people I know
run their index fingers
along scars from puncture wounds
      in the 8th grade.
they ride around with their fingers
on a trigger—
shoot at people
      Might run,
        Might not.
They wear cell-bar jackets
    and sit in cells on the hottest day of the year
sweating tears into a pillow.
Whose grandmas sit in a window
      waiting for it to rain,
        will it come?
They hold grips on invisible bars
set in place as stripes
coursing through
their hopes and dreams.
Were dreamers,
  that became dreamless
    so that somebody new
    could have them too.
They are girls in buffalo stances,
  that dance for men they hate,
    who even sometimes hate themselves,
    but still paint the pain on in the morning
The people I know
    were young once—
still sag their pants
    and might still hit somebody up,

or shake up with a shorty
outside of a corner store on Chicago.
They're people
who let their childhoods blur
into middle-age, used to wait
outside of random apt. buildings
for someone to leave—so they
could rush in eight deep
and smoke blunts in the boiler room.

The people I know
have flaws, smoke squares,
want to quit, but they haven't
        might not ever.
They bite their fingernails
when they get nervous,
sometimes raw, until it hurts
to hold things
  or press buttons on a phone.
They live in moods,
   illiterate blends of feeling
     emotion empty
       and wet.
Love a certain woman but
whose real girlfriend is sorrow
   and they're getting married in the fall.

They eat propaganda
and throw up lies,
  got holes in their bodies,
     holes in their ideologies.
Join movements—to meet girls
then leave to become Jesus
    in another.
Once invested their futures
  in a little white girl,
    or the Big Bad Boy—

You know what that is—
Bobby? Bobby?

They are dying constellations
    whose genius staggers,
and make decisions
in lines drawn from tumult.
The perpetuity
of an ever-bending arc
throughout the history
    Of our universe.

That find and forget God everyday.
They will live in the jungle,
    and burn down the zoo.
The God and morality inside of them
overpowered by the gorilla.
They can't see far
but can taste a whole universe,
    and can smell the money on you.

Who hurt thinking about
What will make them ache
when they get older.
They never thought
    they'd live past thirty,
      now they are scared to die,
        and want to live forever.

The people I know
go to bed in a cell
but live in whole scenarios
    in lives all around the world
Generations of crooks
  whose DNA are the only fragments
  of matter that matter
  in the bricks of these walls.

Stopped expecting friends
to be there when they got out.
Stopped using the phone
because no one would answer it anyways.
because they remind them
of a time when
they weren't so important—so together.

People I know
wreck their bodies
for prison basketball championships
and smuggle ingredients
through metal detectors
just to eat
  Like human beings.

They are the children
of Armageddon
with teal striated
    in the texture
      of their skin,
and are ready for rapture
who have died
and come back to life
    to move and drift
      like smoke
        forever.

▪ ▪ ▪

For Zeke, writing is a way to preserve his sanity, his humanity. He writes:

> Writing gave me a voice. It made me a writer, a student, a man, an individual outside statistics hidden somewhere. It made me a better son; able to replant seeds over the things I tore down a long time ago.

▪ ▪ ▪

Writing became a way to work through his considerable grief, to make sense of his own narrative and to alter it by retelling it. He tells me that writing is the only thing that hasn't been stolen from him. Still, it also reminds him of his powerlessness. Despite his accomplishments as a writer, and the pride that the Department of Corrections, including the commissioner, takes in those accomplishments, Zeke often finds himself without access to a typewriter or word processor. An unexpected stint in a county jail left him even without a pen. His current job assignment is to fold mylar balloons in an overnight shift. He then sleeps through the precious typing hours that are available to him in the computer lab. Like Chris, he acknowledges that the education he has received as well as the recognition of being a published writer does not ameliorate the realities of incarceration. He writes:

> I will note that even through the experience of being a writer and accomplishing some of the things I have, I still feel very much the enclosure of these places. I haven't been insulated from the anger and the loss and in many ways a gnawing bitterness. The actuality of encagement is harder now to grasp than it ever was.

· · ·

Zeke is not only a writer; he is a student of writing and he invariably finds himself in violation of the ten-book limit that the prison imposes on each prisoner. He doesn't want to be known as an outstanding prison writer; he wants to be known as an outstanding writer, "period."

He believes that his words and the critical and affective reception they garner will allow him to travel to places he can't yet go. It is a freedom of movement, a carpet ride of prose. His work is an imperative; it demands attention even as he is ignored.

Perhaps most importantly, and the reason why he allows his work to appear in this volume, his words, which no bars can hold, force us to think collectively about the ways in which human capital languishes in the name of just punishment. I think of not only the written words of these four writers, but of the millions of words that remain unwritten by so many of their fellow incarcerated men.

These four writers, diverse in background, perspective, personality, education, and criminal history, have more than incarceration in common. They have zealously pursued education on the inside, have been admittedly seduced by the power of reading and writing, and have begun to reframe their sense of themselves. They experience, firsthand and long-term, the brutality of the carceral state, yet in their writing they waste no breath declaring their innocence or defending their crime. They are well aware of the complex factors—sociological, political, familial, and psychological—that led them to prison. There are several aspects about their narratives that are important to emphasize as we consider the relationship between education and incarceration.

Intelligence, Aptitude, Talent

All four of these writers represent what we might call incarcerated intelligence. They are talented. A reader might, with some justification, accuse me of a kind of exceptionalism. This isn't what most of the incarcerated are like. The prison guards remind me that I and the other prison teachers see "the cream of the crop." They are indeed self-selected, a particular segment of the prison population, motivated by the desire to learn, to read, to write. The guards also tell me that when they are in class they are on their best behavior, that I wouldn't believe what some of them are like back on the cellblock. I say that is only proof of an elemental, mundane truism of human interaction as well as a critical rudimentary lesson for all teachers, regardless of content. We reflect the way we are treated in the way we treat others. In the classroom, the incarcerated feel respected and valued. It is not rocket science to figure out why they might be more cooperative, respectful, even civil in that environment as opposed to how they might respond to those whose responsibility it is to keep them constrained, restrained, controlled.

Issues of Mental Health

It would be no exaggeration to say that most of the men with whom I work experience some form of depression, radical mood swings, anxiety, despair. What is tricky is to try to sort out any causal or correlational relationships. Zeke says he fell in love with the grays and his depression led him to the series of self-destructive choices that landed him in prison. Chris's moods are notably mercurial. LaVon is sometimes too ambitious in plans for the future that might never materialize. Fong withdraws like a turtle into a shell of hopelessness and despair that threatens to replace his natural softness with hardness. Did these men and their fellow prisoners have undiagnosed and untreated mental illnesses that led them to prison? Or is it impossible for anyone regardless of their entering state of mental health to stay sane in prison?

This latter question has significant implications for the role of education and literacy in prison. If we decide, as a society, to keep people in prison and alive, what responsibility do we have to maintain their health, both physical and mental, and their humanity? For all four of these men, and for many of the others with whom I worked, education can keep them sane and on an even keel.

Lack of Interest in School Prior to Incarceration

All four of these incarcerated writers demonstrated a keen and impressive desire to learn, yet high school failed to engage all four of them for different reasons. None of these four were classified as special-needs learners or segregated into special education, as many of the incarcerated are, yet school failed to capture their interest (Mader & Butrymowicz, 2014).

The next chapter considers some of the reasons why school failed to engage these learners and how schools are implicated in the incarceration of these men and hundreds of thousands of others.

Sticks and Stones

Last week, the students turned in their "Sticks and Stones" essay. Here were the directions for the essay:

"Sticks and Stones" Essay

We've all heard the saying "Sticks and stones may break my bones, but names may never harm me." Yet most of us have experienced the power of language to harm us.

Write a personal essay of 2–3 typewritten or 3–4 handwritten pages where you recall an incident where you were either the target of hurtful language or you were the instigator.

Make certain that in your essay you discuss:

- the incident itself, including the participants, the history, and the language involved
- the personal, social, historical, and cultural reasons why the language was so hurtful
- the consequences of the use of that language
- your current reflections on the significance of the incident

Your essay should be titled. Please proofread for punctuation, spelling, and paragraphing.

We arranged ourselves in a big misshapen circle, and each student was asked to speak about what he wrote, although they did have the opportunity to pass, and two or three did. One by one, the students described a time, sometimes from early childhood, sometimes from the time they have spent in prison, when words created hurt. Several students described the first time they heard the "n" word; others from the opposite side of the circle confessed to when they first used it. Ross talked about hearing the word "white boy." As he described his early childhood in a foster home, we could see his classmates soften toward him. Victim stories and perpetrator stories were about evenly split. We also got several incarceration stories—the incident that landed them in prison or the incident that foreshadowed the incident that landed them in prison.

The class felt like a group meeting. There were tears, and there was laughter. Two students discovered they had both used the same title "Why Me?" and chuckled about it. Everyone listened to one another's stories with an earnestness and an empathy that they didn't always demonstrate for their opposing political and intellectual positions.

Several students took us up on our invitation to experiment with nontraditional forms. Ezekiel wrote a short story; Terrell wrote a poem. The pain, hurt, and anger rose from nearly every page like storm clouds. Many expressed contrition, shame, and embarrassment. Two asked that we not share their work in any way because what they wrote was simply too painful. "It's for your eyes only, as my teachers," one wrote.

Others were eager to share their stories. They want people to know that they have been hurt. They want people to know that they have changed. They want people to know that they are sorry for the hurt they have caused. They want people to know that they have learned that language is power and that they learned that the hard way.

Jason wrote about the day he learned his mother died. Check out his note of apology at the bottom of the page—he wasn't sure his essay fit the assignment.

> Looking back on it now, those words impacted my life more than any others because of the turn-for-the-worst that my life would take after that day. After that day I just continued to spiral downward until I reached prison. Without my mom to guide me, I was on my own. I ended up having to live with my dad, and he continued to not be around much. Ever since that day I've basically been just lost trying to find my way on my own.
>
> A lot of the mistakes that I've made can be attributed to not having the guidance and structure that my mom would have provided. I know that

had she not died, I would not be in prison right now, and I definitely wouldn't be heavily tattooed. That sentence or two affected my life deeper than someone calling me cracker or honky ever could.

The words that were used to tell me that my mom had died were a lot more than just words. Those words were a turning point towards the rest of my life.

(Handwritten note of apology)

I wrote about a situation that hurt me the most with words. If you'd like me to rewrite the paper about a situation involving insult, just let me know. I'll be happy to do it.

Joe mourns the loss of a relationship, swearing he has changed:

The pain that has resulted from these words still echoes through me to this day. The effect of severing communications—which these words represent—has created a chasm between us that I can find no way to circumnavigate, and trust me I have tried. I have spent sleepless nights pondering why such an obstacle even exists, and I have come to realize that the true travesty in this situation is that the man that she was angry with, does no longer exist—for the fact is I have changed, but sadly, now she has no way of knowing this. If we cannot communicate, I have no way of conveying or proving that today I am not the same man I was yesterday. And every morning when I awake, I say a prayer that one day she will allow me to speak with her and with my children once again.

Jon remembers the racial slurs on the playground of his St. Paul youth:

We Could Have Been Friends

Have you ever seen an Asian man as a main character in a movie in which he wasn't portrayed as knowing martial arts, being a homosexual, or a perverted nerd? Ever since I was born these media stereotypes of Asian males are all that I've seen and heard in mainstream America. From today's Jackie Chan to the days of Charlie Chan this skewed image has been reinforced over and over again. At times they didn't even let an Asian man play an Asian man in the movies. So it is no surprise that growing up I was always bombarded with the question, "Do you know kung fu?" or "Do you know karate?" Along with that I'd also get a Bruce Lee esq "Whaaw!" and a karate chop in the air. The most offending things to ever happen to me didn't come from a movie or a question. This incident happened to me on the joyful and sometimes cruel playground of my neighborhood.

And Brian eloquently recounts a harsh interaction with his stepmother over his grades, claiming that at that moment, he began to spiral into the person who would land in prison for life:

I felt the stings there on my bed, and I continued to feel those lashes for a long time after the eruption. My state of mind had to be rebuilt, and a new cornerstone had to be carved out of a new ideology. What once was, was no more. It was difficult to decipher that all of this devastation took place over a couple of letters on a piece of paper that didn't constitute how hard I strived to do my best, and not just academically.

As I look back on this important piece of my childhood, I realize how vulnerable I was to all types of attacks, and part of it may have to do with that ambient innocence of a child. Even now I am vulnerable to verbal attacks because I take everything directed at me to heart; as I've stated before, I wear my heart on my sleeve, unarmored, and statements weigh heavily on my mind thoroughly before discarded. Because of what was said that day, the gap between my step-mother and me grew into a canyon, and any unkind words that were said from then on had to float across that chasm and came to me only as echoes. It's a feeling that I never want to feel again and I never want to make another person, especially one that I care dearly for, have to experience that agony. I realize the importance of the way we talk to each other and communicate with one another, and how damaging taboo language and hate speech can be. The consequences go far beyond that of physical injury; the harm can be irreparable and one's psyche and emotional wellbeing can experience severe affliction. The wound may scab over, but a ghost of that wound could always haunt the heart and mind. I don't think talk is cheap; on the contrary, it comes at a very high price.

Those wounds do continue to haunt, but perhaps writing and talking about them provides an opportunity for both reflection and healing.

CHAPTER SEVEN

"What If I Had Started to Write in High School?"

INTERRUPTING THE SCHOOL-TO-PRISON PIPELINE

SOME DAYS I FIND MYSELF moving from an urban public school during the day to the prison in the evening. On those days, I can't stop thinking about the two populations simultaneously. When I am at a high school and I see a young man with his head down on a desk, or detained in the front office, or given a severe scolding by an administrator, or hanging out in the stairwell, I flash to the men before me in my prison class and wonder what can be done to ensure that these high school students don't end up there. Conversely, when I am at the prison, I try to look beyond the weathered and resigned men I see, those who have been incarcerated for ten or twenty years, even though some of them have not yet reached their fortieth birthday. What were they like in high school, I wonder? When did they commit their first offense? What, if anything, might have kept them in school and out of prison? To be sure, teaching these incarcerated men, offering them the value of liberal arts education and the opportunity to express themselves through writing, seems to me to be the most important thing I can do. I hope that the previous chapters of this volume have made a strong case for why educational opportunities for the currently incarcerated are imperative. Still, the men themselves urge me to think of their "little brothers" who have not yet been caught in the web of the criminal justice system. "There really isn't any hope for me," one of these incarcerated men recently told me. "I will leave here in a pine box. I want you to reach out to those high school kids while there is still time."

During the decade in which I was a high school teacher, I worked with students whom I thought were walking a tightrope between going to college and going to jail. They were smart but disengaged in school. They were interesting, good young people who managed to get into trouble frequently. They often had complicated home lives. Their peer groups included youth who were doing even worse in school than they were. They didn't necessarily see themselves as college material, nor, to be honest, did most of their teachers.

Until I began volunteering in the prison, my teaching life, first as a public-school English teacher and later as a college professor, insulated me so that I'd only seen the students who ended up in college. Now I see the other side, the ones who were not caught by the "catchers in the rye" we teachers sometimes fancy ourselves to be. Now I see the ones who were harmed rather than helped by a system that contributed to their senses of failure and their self-images as outlaws.

I think every schoolteacher should be a prison teacher, at least for a while. Although, as a high school teacher, I congratulated myself for the sense of urgency I felt about working with students who were in danger of leaving school, that urgency would have been fueled by a more acute knowledge of what might await them. There are students in my prison classes who were picked up at their high school by the police, who committed crimes as fifteen-year-old runaways, who have moved from foster home to juvenile detention facility to a maximum-security prison, who have grown from boys to men—in prison. Many of them are serving life sentences, with no possibility of parole, for crimes they were found guilty of while they were still adolescents. Yet they are avid readers and writers with keen intellectual appetites that were not fed in the high schools they sporadically attended, dropped out of, or were expelled from.

One evening in my Introduction to Literature class at the prison, as I was passing back interpretive essays on James Baldwin's "Sonny's Blues," I stopped at Zeke's desk and said, "This paper is amazing. You are a terrific writer. Where did you learn to write like that? Where did you go to high school?"

"South High in the '90s."

"I was there," I exclaimed. "I never saw you."

"That's probably because I never went to class," he said. "And it's too bad, because maybe if I had, I wouldn't be here now."

In that moment, I found myself wondering what might have happened if Zeke *had* been in one of my classes. Did I really believe that an appealing English class and an interested teacher would have made all the difference in the life of an urban youth with two loving parents, prone to depression, chemical use, and peer pressure? Of course not. The path to incarceration is too complex to be interrupted by a single positive educational experience. Besides, that kind of thinking leads dangerously to the teacher-as-heroine mind-set made popular by books and films such as *Freedom Writers* or *Dangerous Minds*. It is not only unrealistic; it is disrespectful and even patronizing for teachers, especially white female teachers, to cast themselves as heroes or saviors, especially of black and brown students in underresourced schools. Buy them a steak dinner at a fancy restaurant, invite them to your middle-class home and make them tea, let them write poetry, and they will stay out of jail. Erica Meiners (2007) reminds us of the insidiousness of this kind of mind-set, what she calls White Lady Bountiful (WLB):

> I focus on the WLB as I view this often unacknowledged identity as a prevalent and persistent icon with significant consequences related to the linkages between schools and jails. . . . WLB (*White Lady Bountiful*) is well represented in Northern American popular culture, perhaps most vividly in the tousled blonde head of Michelle Pfeiffer, who saves "at-risk" students (urban youths of color) by taking them out for expensive dinners in the Hollywood film *Dangerous Minds* (1995). (p. 49)

Nevertheless, public schools do play a significant role in the path of young people to incarceration. As Meiners points out:

> If the foundation of teaching is intimately connected to forms of race-, class-, gender-, and sexuality-based surveillance, it seems more than plausible that we continue to reproduce versions of this

surveillance today. Teachers, scaffolded by institutional policies and norms that work to mask how schools support other systems and attempt to erase race, move youth from schools to jails. (p. 49)

As I will explore in more detail in this chapter, schools are complicit in a variety of ways in moving youth from school to prisons. But they could play a significant role in keeping them out of prison. I stand here with my incarcerated students at the end of the school-to-prison pipeline, with so many of them tried as juveniles and given life sentences, and I wonder how the arc of these promising lives, gone so wrong, might have been altered. I think it is imperative to map their journey backward from the prison to the schoolhouse to see what factors in their educational experiences contributed to their incarceration.

The school-to-prison pipeline or nexus is one of the most urgent educational issues of our time, yet it has received little systematic attention by researchers and educators who could actually reframe curriculum and policy. Many scholars and youth advocates contend that the overpolicing of urban schools, racial profiling of "at-risk" students, zero-tolerance disciplinary policies leading to suspensions and expulsions, and low academic expectations for certain students create a direct pipeline to our nation's prison system. While some of my incarcerated students in our classes did receive decent educations, many testify to a difficult school experience that only amplified their challenges at home.

School disciplinary policies in the United States continue to rely on punitive practices that disproportionately marginalize youth of color and other historically underserved populations (Noguera, 2003). These policies have sent hundreds of thousands of children down life paths that lead to arrest, conviction, and incarceration, resulting in the so-called pipeline that some have argued is a modern form of resegregation that echoes the Jim Crow laws of our recent past (Alexander, 2012). A 2005 publication of the NAACP Legal Defense and Education Fund, "Dismantling the School to Prison Pipeline," puts it this way:

In the last decade, the punitive and overzealous tools and approaches of the modern criminal justice system have seeped into our schools, serving to remove children from mainstream educational environments and funnel them onto a one-way path toward prison. These various policies, collectively referred to as the School-to-Prison Pipeline, push children out of school and hasten their entry into the juvenile, and eventually the criminal, justice system, where prison is the end of the road. Historical inequities, such as segregated education, concentrated poverty, and racial disparities in law enforcement, all feed the pipeline. (2005, p. 2)

There are several kinds of factors that implicate schools in the future eventual incarceration of their students. First, a failing public school is often "the entry point to the school-to-prison pipeline" (p. 4, NAACP, 2005). Communities that are already deeply affected by both poverty and crime are often the site of neighborhood schools that are unable to help the children who attend them to have a positive educational experience, one that decreases rather than increases the likelihood of incarceration. Rundown physical facilities, a high turnover rate of often inadequately trained teachers, lack of curricular resources including current textbooks, and the incorporation of draconian disciplinary practices in the name of "school safety," can all become contributing factors in the school-to-prison pipeline. As the NAACP report points out:

Specifically, fewer resources and attention to students yield poor educational achievement and poor behavioral outcomes. The inadequacies of the public educational system, especially in areas of concentrated poverty, have set students up to fail, as continuing resource deficiencies—evidenced by a lack of experienced or certified teachers and guidance counselors, advanced instruction, early intervention programs, extracurricular activities, and safe, well equipped facilities—lock many students into second-class educational environments that neglect their needs and make them feel disengaged from their schools. Many schools that are labeled as "failing" or even "dangerous" simply do not receive the inputs they need to promote a healthy, sustainable educational environment. As a result, the negative labels placed upon both schools and students become self-fulfilling prophecies. (2005, p. 5)

In addition to the state of the underresourced schools from which many of the incarcerated arrive, there is often a general lack of engagement with learning that many of my incarcerated students, even the most intellectually engaged, report. In one of my first prison classes, I asked students to complete a literacy timeline to track the kind of reading that they did both in and out of school before they were incarcerated. Despite the fact that nearly all of the students considered themselves to be avid readers, many of them confessed to never having finished an entire book before they entered prison. Most of them remarked that the required reading was boring or irrelevant and they just simply didn't do the assigned homework. The incarcerated students reflected much of what we have learned in recent literacy research about the importance of providing literary texts that reflect the realities of the lives of the students. Recent research on adolescent response to literature reveals that when students see themselves reflected in the texts that are assigned, they are more likely to complete assignments and experience more academic success. Additionally, students need to be able to connect their lived experiences as well as their content knowledge to the texts they are asked to read in school (Smith and Wilhelm, 2002; Tatum, 2005; Tatum, 2009). The incarcerated students with whom I work frequently commented that had they encountered more engaging content when they were in middle and high school, they might actually have done the work.

Similarly, students reported very little opportunity to express themselves through any kind of writing during secondary school, especially creative writing. This lack of writing is consistent with recent reports on the state of writing in secondary schools, such as *The Neglected R.* (National Commission on Writing in America's Schools and Colleges, 2003). While the report states that most students have mastered the most basic and rudimentary aspects of writing, they do not have enough opportunity to use writing to express complex thoughts and responses:

> There are many students capable of identifying every part of speech who are barely able to produce a piece of prose. While exercises in descriptive, creative, and narrative writing help develop students'

skills, writing is best understood as a complex intellectual activity that requires students to stretch their minds, sharpen their analytical capabilities, and make valid and accurate distinctions. . . . As a nation, we can barely begin to imagine how powerful K–16 education might be if writing were put in its proper focus. Facility with writing opens students up to the pleasure of exercising their minds in ways that drilling on facts, details, and information never will. More than a way of knowing, writing is an act of discovery. (pp. 13–14)

In addition to not being able to fully develop their literacy skills, the incarcerated students report that because they rarely were asked to express their opinions or their responses and reactions to both academic and personal topics, they felt that those opinions and reactions were not valued. The cumulative effect of this was that they felt that they themselves were not valued or important members of the class. It became easier to not attend class than to attend it and feel ignored or, worse, marginalized.

Perhaps one of the strongest aspects of education as both rehabilitation and liberation is to offer students the opportunity to express themselves and to recraft their personal narratives in their own words. Through creative writing, students are able to connect the acts of literacy to their own experiences. The lack of these opportunities for so many of them stands in marked contrast to the degree to which prison writing has become an important literary art form as well as an avenue of healing for the incarcerated. In lamenting access to computer time caused by a shift in work schedule, one writer recently exclaimed, "Being able to write is what keeps me alive and sane. I don't know what I would be able to do without it."

If the curriculum in our secondary schools included more authentic learning opportunities that drew on students' prior knowledge, integrated texts that had relevance to students' lived experiences, and afforded disenfranchised and disengaged students opportunities to express themselves, perhaps some students might have experienced earlier the kind of enthusiasm for learning that they discover once they are behind bars.

I am reminded of a Gary Soto story called "The Pie"—one of my incarcerated students' favorites. In the telling of a childhood incident that involves the theft of a pie, Soto writes "Boredom made me sin." Many students, bored in and by school, end up being suspended or even expelled and find themselves on the streets and in trouble.

Thus far, we have discussed some of the structural aspects of secondary schooling that fail to engage many young people. However, it is generally not an uninspiring curriculum or a dilapidated school building that is cited as the primary component of the school-to-prison pipeline; it is a series of disciplinary policies. These disciplinary policies, draconian and too often disproportionately involving youth of color, implicate schools in the mass incarceration that Michelle Alexander has called the New Jim Crow. In fact, in addition to the United States incarcerating more adults than any other nation in the world, the "US imprisons more young people at a higher rate than any other nation" (Aizer and Doyle, 2013). Many scholars have drawn direct lines from particular disciplinary practices in high schools to the life trajectory of those who end up in our nation's prisons.

Zero-Tolerance Policies

Among the chief elements of these kinds of disciplinary approaches are what is frequently called zero-tolerance policies. These policies remove students from school decisively, often after relatively minor infractions. There are several significant issues with zero-tolerance policies.

First, they have been shown to disproportionately affect black and brown youth. According to an article in *Juvenile and Family Justice Today*:

> A study of the impact of zero tolerance policies shows "that minority youth are disproportionately suspended and referred to court on school related offenses. Black students are 2.6 times as likely to be suspended as White students. For example, in 2000, Black students represented 17% of the nation's student population yet represented 34% of the suspended population. There is no evidence connecting this disparity to poverty or assumptions that youth of color are prone to disruptive and violent behavior. On the contrary, studies indicate

that this overrepresentation of Black students is related to referral bias on the part of school officials. (Teske and Huff, 2011, p. 15)

Policing School Hallways

Additionally, there has been a dramatic increase of police presence in high schools. In her ethnographic study, *Police in the Hallways*, Kathleen Nolan (2011) is careful not to blame the presence of police in the hallways of high schools and other disciplinary practices for the difficult life course of the young people she studied. She urges us to "look beyond the school into the lives of low-income urban youth and their social and economic reality to have any real sense of their struggles and the logic of their choices" (p. 182). Nolan does well to point out that schools cannot be blamed for the complex issues youth face that often lead to their incarceration. Still, school is indeed implicated in the life trajectory of young people in a number of ways. Nolan writes:

> Perhaps the most important insight that emerged from the study is that within the framework of zero tolerance and order maintenance, students end up getting summoned to criminal court for incidents that began with a minor school rule, not the law. (2011, p. 163)

She continues:

> The heavy policing of low-income youth of color in and out of school is perhaps one of the most potent reflections of the ethos of exclusion that inspires today's policies. Zero tolerance and order maintenance are striking examples of our societal response to social problems caused by inequality and poverty. (p. 182)

The presence of police in schools has been demonstrated to have serious negative effects on some students, most especially black and brown students. Additionally, these youth are often removed from the school in handcuffs. Referrals to courts jump significantly, sometimes more than 1000%, when police are present in schools. A student arrested in school is twice as likely not to graduate and four times as likely not to graduate if he or she appears in court (Teske and Huff, 2011).

Early Court Involvement and Detention

Many of my incarcerated students entered the prison system as court-involved youth. Several of them made their first court appearances at the ages of fifteen or sixteen. A few of them knew one another from juvenile detention centers, met again in a prison designed for youth, and finally landed in the same high-security prison where I teach. Perhaps it is too obvious to state, but it seems clear that early court involvement dramatically increases the likelihood of later incarceration. In a study on the societal costs of incarcerating juveniles, economists Aizer and Doyle (2013) write:

> Our results suggest that incarcerating juveniles, at tremendous cost, serves to reduce their educational attainment and increase the probability of incarceration as an adult. In sum, keeping students from entering the juvenile justice system is an important step in curbing the flow of the school-to-prison pipeline and making sure they can get their lives back on track. Diversion programs help keep youth out of the system, and these programs work best when youth are diverted before they're even arrested. (Conclusions, para. 1)

Understanding the contributing factors of the school-to-prison pipeline is clearly insufficient. From the end of the pipeline it seems urgent to find ways of keeping youth in school and out of prison. I listen to my incarcerated students, especially those serving life sentences, telling me that my efforts should focus on how to keep others from joining them in prison. There are a variety of initiatives, both in and out of schools, designed to do just that.

First, several urban school districts have adopted a teacher-recruitment program called "Grow Your Own." This program is designed to recruit teacher candidates from communities, especially communities of color, and then return to teach in those communities.

Teachers who have a stake in the community, who understand the various challenges that young people may face in that community, and who, not incidentally, may share the same heritage as the students they teach, might be in a unique position to work effectively with youth from that community who might identity with them. According to Eric Duncan (former Lee Public Policy Fellow, US Department of Education), students are positively impacted by teachers who know the students, know the community, and know the history of the community. Duncan describes the importance of Grow Your Own teacher-recruitment programs this way:

> "Students need to see people (in front of the classroom) who come from where they come, who look like them and act like them. It's an important cultural shift." (Zuber & Berg-Jacobson, 2017)

In addition to changing the nature of the teaching force, some schools have adopted programs that employ restorative justice rather than punishment. In *Justice on Both Sides: Transforming Education Through Restorative Justice* (2018), Maisha Winn calls for a paradigmatic shift in how schools can address issues of inequity and injustice without resorting to the kinds of punitive approaches that can move youth from schools to prison. She writes:

> "Restorative justice is not merely an alternative to punishment; it is a way of life, and it can be difficult to ignore our instinct and not determine in advance whether someone is worthy of our attention and grace" (p. 18).

Winn outlines an approach to restorative justice practices that involves students, teachers, and administrators in a collective effort to transform schools from places of pain and punishment to sites of healing and transformation.

At an urban high school in the Midwest, a principal has eschewed traditional approaches to discipline in his majority-nonwhite high school for a shared system of governance whereby the students not only do not break rules, they actually have a hand in making rules. The focus of this innovative program is, as Winn calls for, not simply a substitute for traditional forms of discipline but a way to build relationships and community with the goal of transforming the overall climate of the school (Lonetree, 2018). Using student-led circles during the first fifteen minutes of each lunch period, the entire school strives to animate the following vision for the school:

> At Johnson Senior High School, we have an unconditional positive regard for all students and staff. We expect everyone entering our building to strive to demonstrate the same unconditional positive regard for all staff and students. This is our culture, and we are committed to helping everyone honor it.

Students and teachers are asked to work toward the following goals and to share the following beliefs:

Goals:
- To make sure that students are fully involved in making more good things happen and fewer bad things happen at Johnson High School every day.
- To ensure that juniors and seniors have multiple opportunities and support to practice leadership in all aspects of the school.
- To build a stronger Johnson community that more fully and quickly integrates our underclass students into the positive school culture and opportunities of Johnson High School.
- To increase the academic success and social integration of all JHS students.

Fundamental Beliefs:
1. What hurts my brother or sister hurts me.
2. We welcome, celebrate, and strive to understand the rich variety of gifts brought to our community by people with diverse cultural and racial backgrounds.
3. Nothing works unless I work. We define success in terms of effort, grit, cooperation, positive school climate, and willingness to try again as much as results on standardized tests.

4. Our school's culture and climate does not simply happen, but is carefully designed and cultivated to accomplish our educational mission.

5. School is not a spectator sport. Our school is like a ship composed entirely of working crew; there are no entitled passengers just along for the ride.

6. Teaching is not the same as telling.

7. Adults should not do for students what students can do for themselves.

8. We must be a safe space—physically and psychologically.

9. We take seriously the need to be positive role models for younger students.

10. Students need as many opportunities as possible to build a positive self-image and a sense of competence.

11. Immediate and real consequences are essential to learning.

12. Academic problems are seldom purely academic; we work to address needs and problems both in and beyond the classroom.

13. We have high expectations for academics and behavior.

14. When we raise expectations, we must also offer the means to meet the new expectations.

This is precisely the kind of paradigmatic shift in culture that Maisha Winn calls for. In the year since the program has begun, student fights and suspensions have dramatically decreased and other schools throughout the state are looking at implementing a similar model.

In addition to transforming disciplinary practices, curriculum may also need to be transformed in order to more fully engage those students who may be vulnerable to getting caught in the pipeline. Following the suggestions of my incarcerated students, I have also been working with teachers in area high schools to help create a curriculum that is more engaging to their urban students. In some cases, the curricular innovation is designed to directly address issues of mass incarceration and the school-to-prison pipeline. In one high school, a teacher assigned ninth graders to read Walter Mosley's adolescent novel, *Always Outnumbered, Always Outgunned*, the story of an older African American man recently released from prison and his relationship with a young

African American male who seems destined to follow the same path of incarceration. In addition to reading and discussing the novel, one of my formerly incarcerated students visited the classes and discussed the reality of incarceration with them.

At another school in Minneapolis, two remarkable teachers have created an extensive unit on issues of incarceration, which include a graphic novel representation of Michelle Alexander's *The New Jim Crow* called *Race to Incarcerate*. They also view and discuss the films *13th* and *The House I Live In*. In yet another school, students studied the issue of mass incarceration in a social studies class. In addition to reading *The New Jim Crow*, they read pieces from the creative writing anthology my incarcerated students published. Then they write letters to the incarcerated writers. It was a rare opportunity for both ends of the pipeline to meet. Here is the response the incarcerated writers sent to the high school students:

The Prison Writers' Collective

Dear Students,

Thank you so much for your letters. We appreciate your responses and depth of insight. We don't get to see the effects of our work too often. With the exception of Mrs. Appleman, we have no idea of the impact our words may have. To be able to see firsthand what you all thought about the project was encouraging.

It really inspires us to know that you are contemplating and reflecting such heavy societal issues. Prison is a place that for many years has remained hidden in the dredges of society. Without projects like the book and classes like Mrs. Appleman's a large portion of people would never understand how damaging poverty can be. Prisons were designed. They were supposed to solve problems, not create more issues. It is only by targeting a voiceless population that such industry was able to sustain for so long. But now, with greater awareness we are able to do something to help those that are broken, hopefully before they hurt anyone else.

We find comfort in the fact that you are reading our words. It makes us believe that we can still make a difference somehow; that our mistakes can be learned from. We hope that they will help you be better people somehow.

Possibly, they can help you avoid some of the hardships that we have endured. But most likely they will show you the human side of the fellow citizens that our society is all too quick to write off and treat as animals.

We are all part of the same community, and we have a social obligation to each other whether we like it or not. We apologize for failing you; for waking up too late. But we thank you for listening to us although we've done nothing to deserve your ear.

Sincerely Yours

In addition to these in-school efforts to help interrupt the school-to-prison pipeline, there are also community efforts, from structured activities in sports facilities to entire leadership programs and community programs that pair young men with elders. One such program in an area of my city that is unfortunately notorious for gang-related activity works diligently to create alternative spaces for youth and to pair them with caring adult mentors. In fact, several of my formerly incarcerated students have now become mentors in this program, using their hard-earned experience from the end of the pipeline to help others from getting caught in it. Here is a description of that program:

The Boys of Hope Program™ is a weekly program designed for boys in grades 6–12. The program is facilitated by men from the community who engage boys in a critical thinking, reflective, hands-on, experiential based process where they explore five core curriculum components: personal power, cultural awareness, manhood, leadership development, and service-learning. The program also engages men from the community as "Social Fathers" to be role models, mentors and career coaches as a core strategy for motivating, inspiring, and educating boys on how to be a positive and productive man in your community. (The Power of People Leadership Institute, 2018)

In sum, it is critically important that we find ways to stop the torrent of young people headed to our nation's jails and prisons. We need to reform what we teach and how we teach it as well as the ways in which young people are treated within the walls of their high schools. As we have seen, the incarcerated men with whom I work feel that it is more important to keep youth out of jail than it is to try to provide educational opportunities to the incarcerated. Our first creative writing anthology was called *From the Inside Out: Letters to Young Men and Other Writing.* It was created so that the incarcerated men could reach out to young men who were in the pipeline but could still get out.

Perhaps those at the end of the pipeline have the most powerful things to say about how to interrupt it. In the spirit of James Baldwin's "Letter to my Nephew," Terelle, or "Twin" as he is known, incarcerated before he was eighteen and serving a long sentence, writes a cautionary tale to his own nephews:

> *Dear Nephews:*
>
> *Despite spending more than a decade in prison I have been watching you both out of love and genuine concern. I have been hearing about your deeds and I am starting to see a pattern in your behavior. It is the same pattern of behavior that mirrored mine's when I was your age. If you do not defer from this pattern of behavior you may find that a visit to prison may very well be in your future. I am quite sure that you do not wish to experience this. There is no nightmare that you can dream that will be more horrible.*
>
> *I worry about you even more now because you have reached the age when young black men enter into a world of social disenfranchisement and other forms of discrimination. Most of your fathers are not in the home so then it becomes a world of displaced and misplaced ideals of manhood which have their origins in pseudo-urban myths and is largely perpetuated by the culture of the mass media. It is a world where if you follow and not lead, peer-pressure will inevitably destroy what you innately can become. Your talents will be wasted engaging in meaningless gang activity, crime, drugs and women. This is the design of a political system diluted with historical, social, and economical intricacies that will lead you to the gates of prison. I have seen this modern-day urban tragedy reoccur time and time again.*
>
> *I entered prison when I was eighteen. The ultimate details of what landed me behind these walls have almost torn this family apart. For years I was frustrated and confused, but the time I spent studying gave me great insight and allowed me to understand the responsibility that I needed to take for my*

own actions, the role the family has played and the role that I nor the family can be held accountable for. We as a family are not totally innocent, because we have failed in the sense that we did not have an overwhelming desire to want something better for ourselves. This is the natural state of man. Hopefully, this letter helps break this vicious cycle. Ultimately, your futures wholly depend on it.

Even though you are children, you have a responsibly [sic] that is virtually impossible to achieve. You have to say no to gangs, crime, drugs and promiscuity. Yet these things dominate your current environment. You must resist them; you have to revolt against an entire cultural system that does not hold your interest at heart. What you will be saying is no to a system that defines these things as a rite of passage into manhood.

Furthermore, you will be left alone to make all the right decisions and if you make the wrong decision you will not be exempt from facing the consequences. This means that in order to survive this decadent culture every one of you will most likely become a product of your environment.

You have to compensate for your own inadequacies and the inadequacies of your mothers and fathers thanks the inadequacies of their mothers and fathers, of your communities and institutions, of your government. You will have to be the visionaries that will be left with the duties to secure your own futures because in the historically previous generations have failed you miserably.

I tell you this not to place a heavy burden up on you but this is the shape and color of our current reality. You are too young to understand that your government on every level debate on how much funding they should cut from the school budget, meanwhile your schools are already under funded and you're already undereducated and miseducated. Federal and state governments believe that building prisons and military spending is more fiscally responsible than educating the nation's youth. They have cut social programs such as the arts, sports and community centers that hone your physical and cognitive abilities. As a direct consequence these viable institutions which sponsor positive mentorship in urban communities' nationwide have been replaced with negative influences from members of street organizations and drug dealing crews.

It is unfortunate that the wrong people are the most willing to take an interest in you. However, these are the people who you must avoid like the plague; these are the very people that will play a major role in the destruction of your futures. Oddly enough, they fill a void that is not being fulfilled in the community and family structure. While millions of young African American men are being led down the wrong path, pragmatic solutions are not being implemented to reverse this negative trend which have literally decimated two generations. This phenomenon is highly unfortunate when young people are in part, a viable asset to a nation's future.

Author Victor Frankl once wrote in his book, Man's Search for Meaning, *that the abnormal becomes normal in abnormal situations. He said this in regards to the millions of Jews who were forced to steal clothes from dead people so they could survive the terror of the concentration camps during the Holocaust. This is currently what's going on in many cities across America; young people are forced to behave abnormally because their forbearers have abandoned them to an existence of atypical conditions.*

I too have abandoned you, not consciously. Very much like you, the day I entered the urban reality I was ignorant of overall society. I responded to the conditions of my environment. I didn't rise above becoming a product when I was given the opportunity, instead I wasted my physical and mental talents to running with gangs and benefitting off of drug profits because I could not see beyond immediate sustainability over long-term sustainability, a mistake that I desperately regret today as I peer out into the world from my cell bars.

However, you have a choice. The choices you have are that you can sacrifice yourself and suffer on the road to achieving the American dream honestly and respectfully which will take time and patience or you can advance your dreams hastily and destructively and without regard for your fellow man. But nonetheless, if you choose the latter there will be consequences for your actions and know that your family and community will suffer to which you are an essential part. In light of this, I will end this letter by asking this of you: always be on guard and do what is right.

I love you deeply.

Sincerely yours,
Your uncle
Terelle

School-to-Prison Pipeline

There is much talk about the school-to-prison pipeline. Briefly, many youth advocates contend that the overpolicing of urban schools, racial profiling of "at-risk" students, zero-tolerance disciplinary policies leading to suspensions and expulsions, and low academic expectations for certain students create a direct pipeline to our nation's prison system for some youth.

While some students in our class did receive decent educations, in both public and private schools, many testify to a difficult school experience that only amplified their challenges at home. LaVon writes of a "miseducation," so commonly experienced by African American males:

> As I grew older I began to learn about myself, who the real me really was. I started educating myself in ways to become a better man, in how to become a so called black man. I started recognizing the miseducation I was receiving from my schools for what it was. It was this misguided message that propelled me to seek knowledge elsewhere.

Chris writes of being misdiagnosed with a speech impediment because of his accent:

> Very early on I was diagnosed by the school as having a speech impediment because they believed that I had an issue pronouncing my R's correctly. I can recall the classes making me feel as though something was wrong with me and added to my insecurities speaking up which in turn developed a mumbling problem. I cannot remember ever feeling as though these "special" classes ever helped. Thinking back, I believe my

lean towards slang was orchestrated to hide my "impediment" and give the appearance that I was in more control.

Many educators have gathered in conferences around the country to begin discussions of "dismantling the school-to-prison pipeline." Schools are beginning to review zero-tolerance discipline policies, how students are sorted into special education, and ways in which negative beliefs about particular students are communicated both verbally and nonverbally.

Some schools are beginning to change both their practices and their cultures. For example, in an admittedly schmaltzy but gutsy move, the Dallas Public Schools tried to change the tone of the discourse around students by having a young African American male serve as their keynote speaker. He began his speech by asking the auditorium of educators, "Do you believe in me?"

It is much more likely that those of you reading this blog can effect change within our current public school system rather than within the walls of a correctional facility. I think awareness of the carceral state needs to be a part of every teacher training program. If I had only known as a high school English teacher what I have learned this past year teaching in the prison.

CHAPTER EIGHT

"Songs from the Genius Child"

WORDS NO BARS CAN HOLD

T HE MOST RECENT CLASS I taught at the prison, Reading Like a Writer, inspired by the Francine Prose book of the same name, was designed to encourage the incarcerated writers to learn about the craft of writing from published writers, to think of writing as joining a conversation of thinkers and writers, a conversation that had gone on for centuries before them and would continue for centuries afterward. To that end, the students were asked to bring in a published piece of writing they admired, one that they thought spoke to them, both as readers and as writers.

Bino, one of the most accomplished and versatile writers in the class, chose the following poem by Langston Hughes:

SONG FOR THE GENIUS CHILD
This is a song for the genius child.
Sing it softly, for the song is wild.
Sing it softly as ever you can -
Lest the song get out of hand.

Nobody loves a genius child.

Can you love an eagle,
Tame or wild?

Can you love an eagle,
Wild or tame?
Can you love a monster
Of frightening name?

Nobody loves a genius child.

Kill him - and let his soul run wild.

"Genius Child" from THE COLLECTED POEMS OF LANGSTON HUGHES by Langston Hughes, edited by Arnold Rampersad with David Roessel, Associate Editor, copyright © 1994 by the Estate of Langston Hughes. Used by permission of Alfred A. Knopf, an imprint of the Knopf Doubleday Publishing Group, a division of Penguin Random House LLC. All rights reserved.

In offering an explanation for his choice, as each student was required to do, Bino said, "Well, first of all, I admire the voices of African American poets, especially those like Langston Hughes who have made it into white literary respectability. [He chuckled.] But most of all, I identify with what the poem is about, and I think identifying with some aspect of what you are reading is the key to becoming a good reader. And I guess what we have been learning in this class is that the key to being a good writer is being a good reader. And I really want to become both.

"So, back to the poem. It ain't like I think of myself as a genius or anything, but I *am* like a wild child, a monster they tried to kill, but I have songs now, songs I have written, songs to share. I think we all do. That's why I love this poem."

This final chapter offers a sampling of the songs of Bino and his fellow incarcerated readers and writers, the "genius" children behind bars. They are words that were unleashed by offering the incarcerated the educational opportunities described in previous chapters of this book. It is important to underscore two particular aspects of those educational opportunities. First, although writing is the most visible manifestation of that educational outreach, my approach was much broader than simply offering outlets for creative writing, valuable as that might be. It always included significant and wide reading. Second, as Berry (2018) and Karpowitz (2017) have also written, the focus of this endeavor was liberal arts education, learning for learning's sake, reading for reading's sake, writing for writing's sake. So perhaps the most useful measure of this work is their words.

Writing Selections

As I have discussed elsewhere (Appleman, 2016, 2013), the challenge of many incarcerated writers is to learn to write less, not more, and to use the best words, not the most words. To that end, they have found the genres of haiku and six-word memoirs to be particularly useful in honing their craft. Here is a sampling of each:

Haiku

Prison is a sad place
Lonely cells in long rows
Don't go to prison
  Terrell

In the corner
Collecting dust
My guitar
  China

Isolated and caged
Without the sun's warm guidance
Feathers stagnating
  Starlin

A mind is a terrible
Thing to waste, but
Not worse than an entire life
  LaVon

Camouflage lizard
No one can see you lick

Your own eyeball

Ross

Six-Word Memoirs

One winter evening, the writers' collective and I held a six-word memoir workshop for the entire prison population who wished to attend. There were about seventy men, and a few staff as well. I co-led the workshop with Chris, with LaVon assisting. A few weeks later, I returned for a meeting. As I walked through my usual sober, stark path, I noticed that the long, dark hallway leading up to the education wing was decorated, yes, decorated, with scores of pieces of paper, on which were written six-word memoirs. I still don't know how the writers pulled it off, but for the month that those pieces of paper were up, the entrance of the education wing was transformed into a literary gallery. Here are a few of them:

She did not keep her promise. *Fong*

Chained by desire to be free. *Sarith*

In dreams, my son feels real. *Dao*

Sunshine captured me. Darkness released me. *Bino*

Thorns stay buried in the redeemed. *Chris*

Is this not a black life? *Will*

Where I'm From Poems

The following poems emerged from an assignment that was adapted from Linda Christensen's terrific book, *Reading, Writing, and Rising Up* (2017). It's an assignment called Where I'm From, based on a poem by George Ella Lyons.

WHERE I'M FROM

Jason

I'm from nowhere.
Created out of the existence of the never-loved.
I'm from the void between love and hate.
The quiet emptiness of nothing.

I'm from the don't cares and never-theres.
The two-faced and always-fake.
I'm from the place in a brain where things you've forgotten go.
The dark life-less place.
I'm from the place of bars and cells.
The black cells of hopelessness.
I'm from prison.

WHERE I AM FROM (INSPIRED BY GEORGE ELLA LYONS)
China

I am from Cluster bombs,
From Agent Orange and Napalms.
I am from the durable yellowish-brown wooden stilts
Of my grandmother's house.
I am from the opium poppies,
Bitter, yellow and sweet.

I'm from saris and sarongs,
From gold and have plenty.
I'm from the study hard and success will follow,
From respect your elders and mind your business.
I'm from giving alms every April, June, July, August
and November.
(Lighting candles and burning incense for prayers)

I'm from where elephants crowd,
Sticky rice and papaya salads.
From warring princes to the fall of a dynasty,
The life my father nearly lost protecting our ancestry.
My past, present and future a kaleidoscope of tragedies.
From the Mekong Delta, White Elephants, Lan Xang
Will forever be a distant memory.
I am from Laos.

WHERE I AM FROM

David

I am from the code, from golden spirals
and rhythmic vibrations.
I am from the Highs and Lows,
from the piercing flame tips
and the burrowing seed.

I'm from braces and second-hand smoke,
overpowered hallways and green carpet.
I'm from plastic crates and spinning vinyl-
not wasted on milk and car seats.
I'm from the vertebrae of a martyr,
hangin' and breakin'
from overpasses and subways.

I am from the stomps of elephant feet,
dragon heart beats
and habitual dreamers.
I'm from the bottom of Buddha's foot
and sacrificial stone stairways to heaven.

I'm from the eagle's wing
and serpent's bite.

I am from strung upside-down fenders
and playing along the watchtower.
I am from PURPLE;
hair, haze and rain.

I am from the soft song of a paper pirate
from the bold & tears of out-growing his first tooth.
I'm from her steps, harmonious scents,
chocolate eyes and peanut butter scales.

I'm from dreaming of RED and waking up BLUE.

I am from spiral codes and rhythmic vibrations,
from where contractions and eruptions rendezvous.

Free Verse

As the incarcerated students read more widely, their own writing begins to reflect their expanding literary horizons. While they sometimes choose to write about their experience of incarceration, as Ross and Fong do, they also, like all poets, write about everyday things like leaves and red wagons, or moths in the prison yard, as do Isaac, Dao, and B. And, as an illustration of the ways in which writing can provide opportunities to express pain and provide healing, Zeke works through his grief in "The Mother's Lament," written after his own mother's sudden passing. Below is a sampling of their free verse poems.

THE MOTHER'S LAMENT – AFTER WILLIAM CARLOS WILLIAMS
Zeke

Sorrow is
my own
garden
where the
flowers
bloom as they
have bloomed
often before but
not
with the bittered thorns
that prick and chap my hands this year.
Forty years I
had with my
husband
eighteen
years I
visited

my son
in prison
the crabapple is
white today
dressing for its
bitter fruit.
Silk
clustering
pedals
heavy the
lilac
branches
and color
some
bushes
violet and
some
pink but
the grief
in my
heart
throbs stronger than they
for though they
were my pride
over many
springs, today I
sleep amidst
them, misre-
membering. 18
years I visited
my son.
Today, I dream he
was young long-
haired-I dreamt he
was free he
whispered to me

that on the other side of the
coiled fence at the edge
of woods bound by
heavy'd chain to the
injuries
of time, he saw
a future with white flowers, some violet
and some pink, a meadow,
where the flowers lie like
plumes of cloud in a cerulean
sky.
I'm
sure I
would
like to
go
there
And fall asleep
in the pillows of those plumes.

PRISON PASTORAL
B.

I once mistook a gray moth
lying at my feet on faded grass
for a blanched butterfly.
Its casual stillness,
wings curved hieroglyphs
steely against the bronzed lawn,
startled me;
everything in prison moves in hunched caution,
flightless but bent on flying.
Did it know this wasn't pasture meant
to land on? Did it know my pale shadow
wasn't an elm, and never could be? Did it know,
no matter how much pretending,

it was a moth? I tried to find answers woven in fine silk
on its quiet wings.
The language was dust.

RELINQUISHED NOTES
Isaac

Words colorful fall leaves
that blow swiftly in the wind
my pencil a nightlight
that keeps my path bright
my thoughts are the fireflies
that I follow as the lines fade
clouds cover the moon
smell of rain overbearing
cracking snap of a branch
nocturnal sounds speak
nature looks for a release
rains is quiet morning sun screams
phrases flow below in a stream
rhyming dewdrops adds splendor
while letters hatch, contemplate
soaring together in form
ends chirp convey enticing melody
sun light wipes away all dark
a page left filled with ink

PRISON IS
Ross

Prison is an ancient hairless cat
Hissing, angry
A disturbing, raw experience

It is a weeping wound
Gaping, unhealed
Bleeding out its poison

It is a cracked fun-house mirror
Confusing, twisted
Deluding its masters

It is an aged stepmother
Pretending, bitter
Smiling at her companion

It is diseased heart
Gutted, ruined
Waiting to beat its last.

And yet . . .

It is an unyielding anvil
Pitiless, cruel
A tool upon which I'm remade

It is a bulky, steel hammer
Destructive, creative
Reshaping my mortal essence

It is a fiery crucible
Scorching, consuming
Burning away all impurities

It is a paint-chipped house of worship
Holy, haunting
Inspiring me to greatness

RED WAGON
Dao

The squeaking wheels of my red wagon made me weep.
Every turn, a soft shriek of help escapes a mouth unseen.

True to my vision, I saw the wagon as an unarmed chariot crumbling under
    true greatness,
Apollo, so I pulled him through mountains of sand, canyons of broken pavement
And past unmoving metal monsters with bright colors, deformed and twisted
    bodies.

My mother ran to me from across the park like a gazelle with all its swiftness
And asked me with peanut buttery breath, why I was crying and I told her:
The squeaking wheels of my red wagon made me weep.

Bino's work is a hybrid of free verse and spoken word. It loses much impact from the stage to the page, but it is still worth offering here:

U WOULDN'T UNDERSTAND
Bino

Skin black as Mississippi
soil. Midnight at high-
noon, we absorb light.
When unchosen
oppressive benefactors
became broiled chicken.
They used to crack whips on southern plantations.
We started to whip crack
in cities segregation.
Communities labeled integrated are race riots waiting.

{Focus Hope.   Yeah right}
Focus Dope.   Better yet.
Focus.   Nope.
How does focus work on a scope?

Cross-hairs fixed on a
balcony.
Cross-hairs on
corner-dwellers.

Picked up, held down,
placed in cellars. Who
are the sellers
of American problems?
American mangled morals
porous as a sponge,
absorb
then drip
reality,
imagination.

In cartoons we're ridiculed ridiculous jokes
Daffy Duck with spittle spraying from enlarged lips.
Tasmanian Devil's incoherent speech.
California Raisins singing and dancing with Temptational two-steps.

> Blaxploitation is
> Sambo going Rambo in
> a Lambo, after doing hand-
> to-hands with an
> undercover in a bando. We
> can't win. Even when we win.
> We can't win.

Silenced for so long we make noise to authenticate our
existence. That's why Riley and Huey couldn't assimilate in
The Boondocks. That's why Django chose a blue suit.
That's why Dolemite rapped before kicking ass.

That's why we absorb the
reality of now
of history,
and
allow our imaginations to
flourish.

A DAY AT THE ZOO
Chris

The sun is a bulb, and it burns
through the build ran at your back.
Quarters drop, the turnstile clicks,
another cog spins the machine that made
these gates, brass tacks, bars protecting both sides.

The cackle of all kinds distract from dangers
you move through with bright eyes,
safe from pitched roofs and driveways,
play-date parents and little league crowds.

A lion yawns far from the lioness
you used to be, willing to hunt, taking care of the cubs.
Carefree nature of creatures small and large,
their curious musings, hoots and howls,
a random roar—all simple expressions of broken
inhibition that ground you, like somehow you belong
among the caged with no place to hide from themselves.

Your feet, tight and worn, remind you
you're here for your family, though
the last stop is for you. We appreciate you
enduring the smells, your patient presence
and for feeding us what was allowed.
Cause after all—what are we without you?

My wings splay and scrape against the glass ceiling
of this dome I entered when I gave up on the sky.
At first I soar, pretending not to see you,
then perch on a faux branch near enough
to share space for those moments. It's okay.

I know you have to go soon. Carry me
in thought. Know I consider the cage
worth being free in your heart—
and it's in that freedom you see in my eyes
while I find the prison on yours where you ask,
What is it you want from me?

You reply—*nothing.*
It's settled so stop acting
like you'd take me home
and I'll stop pretending it's possible.

I can never be anything more
than your favorite animal in this zoo.

Memoir and Creative Nonfiction

In addition to poetry, the incarcerated writers choose prose to explore childhood memories, to create portraits of family members they can no longer see frequently and to ruminate on the past and consider the future.

MY MOTHER AND MY MOM
Charles

Though it took me months until we were properly introduced, I've known her the moment my mind took on consciousness. I enjoyed sharing each sweet, spicy, and sour taste she fed us every day. I knew it when she was excited. I knew it when she was sad. Every day I was forced to listen to her 80's soft rock bands and whenever I couldn't take it anymore, I gave her a good kick in the gut from the inside out. The first conversation with her consisted of a lot of screaming and crying from the both of us. We met officially on May 13th, 1984.

Strong, strict, and stubborn, she is my mother. Stout, stern, and short-tempered, I knew her always too quickly to bring down her hand in rage or frustration. I thought of fear from when I thought of my mother. If she were a color, it'd be red, hot and bright like coals against a hearty gust of wind. Deceptively, she stands a mere 4'9, 130 lbs. A woman of small physical stature, her authority is apparent by her commanding voice, like a page from a prison's intercom system echoing up and down the galleys.

In all my years excluding those instances where I've unexpectedly awakened her from her sleep, I've never known my mother not to have on her face and her attire properly squared. Her flamboyant taste in gaudy jewelry, artificially blackened hair—thinning and damaged from years of multiple dying and re-dyings and crimson lips covered always with too much lipstick betray her vanity. The tattooed-on eyebrows made it so she always looked perfectly groomed though her painted nails and toes more than often needed some touching up. Loud, arrogant, and obnoxious, this is the mother my siblings and I was the most familiar with growing up.

Amongst guests and whilst entertaining company, she is comfortably charming and articulate. Often humorous, her distinct laughter is noticeably recognizable anywhere within an earshot. And matched with a smile so wide her eyes are forced closed and teeth off-white and crooked as scoliosis, she appears often quite loveable. Intelligent, clever and resourceful, she always seems to know how to remedy a problemed situation.

Abstained from smoking and drinking, a hard worker, my mother prides herself a great cook. I've never known another more prideful than her, not only of herself but of her possessions. Through her children, she kept the house clean and tidy, dishes washed and laundry always done. She allowed not one of us to leave the house to school with snot still in our eyes or our hair unkempt, our garments in disarray. In her eyes, she made **no** mistakes. Once, she took work off, picked me up from school and drove us 45 minutes to a dentist appointment one week early. She was furious, neither at the receptionists nor the dentist nor even at her own scheduling mishap but at me, for not having remembered the correct date of my appointment, which had been previously scheduled by her six months prior. She then proceeded to give me a 45 minute lecture back to school on how hard *she* works and how it was *my* responsibility to check-up on the dates of all *my* appointments and if there were any discrepancies discovered that *I* was supposed to have let *her* know in advance so this sort of stuff didn't happen. I was 7 years old. I cried all the way back to school.

"I love you," was not spoken in our house. Perhaps due to my culture's conservative attitude towards affection or perhaps saying the words exposed some vulnerability in her to a degree. Brought up Catholic, she snuck in the bible and its stories to us past my father's objections that a White man should worship a White god and a Hmong, Hmong gods. I vaguely remember her tucking me in at night and coaxing me to pray to God before her style of disciplining soon drowned out the remnants of those infantile practices. Although the words were not spoken, according to her, I felt her love whenever she cracked her whip on my backside. "If I hadn't cared, I wouldn't have yelled at you or wasted the time beating you," she'd love to remind me after having just told me how much she hated me, wished I were dead, had been aborted before I were born and my skin were swollen scarlet from the welts she'd dealt me. Where the physical blows did not reach, the emotional ones were cripplingly traumatizing like a veteran scarred with PTSD. Why wasn't my mother like the ones I saw on television, like momma *Brady-Bunch*, Marge Simpson or that mom from *The Little House on the Prairie*?

In my own inherited arrogance I occasionally questioned whether she really loved me or were merely providing for me by law. It wasn't until I was an adolescent that I began to understand her style of love somewhat better. From opaque to vague, it came that I realized how tolling ten hour workdays five times a week taxed her, how costly expensive it is to clothe my five siblings and me, feed us, shelter us, medically insure us and still cook us great stomach fulfilling meals each and every night. Then, I caught *this* case. Sure, I'd been incarcerated before but never having faced a sentence so fatally lengthy.

My mom is loving. She is sensitive, sincere, and so soft. She cries. I've never before seen her shed tears. I actually believed she possessed no tear ducts under those bags beneath her brown eyes. So many facets to her, either she is a great liar, a con, or she's a magician and a master keeper of secrets. Funny, how after a quarter of a century you think you know someone only to be taken aback, surprised still.

It's been almost a year now since last we've seen one another in the visiting room up here at the prison. She requests more frequent visitations except I won't allow them as long as she continues to weep for me throughout our time spent together. I call her every other weekend and find it hilarious how soft spoken she is to me one second and then tells me to hang-on another so as to set down the receiver to devour, demean and devastate those still at home with her. She'd put drill sergeants to shame.

Before this experience, when I thought of my mother, I thought of the hurt and the misery she germinated in my life. Now when I think of my mom, I see how old I've made her, of the hurt and misery I've caused to grow in her. The white hairs from stressing and the discoloration beneath the rim of her eyes obviously display countless sleepless nights on my behalf. I've so much love for this woman. I now remember that night she stayed up caring for me feeding me ice cream when I had my tonsils removed. I remember her teaching me a game with rocks and hand-eye coordination she learned when she were a little girl. I remember staying up late with mom waiting for dad to come home from work, watching late-night horror movies and cuddled up in a single blanket together both too afraid to answer the door when dad came a-knockin'.

I've come to see now the impact she's had on my life, not only in raising me but in who I've become as a person. I look in the mirror and I see so many of the same traits I listed for both resenting and respected her: strength, stubbornness, vanity, short-temperedness, intelligence, pride, honor, humor, the list goes on.

V.X.Y. is my mother and my mom. I see now she is a rainbow of colors. I apologize for misunderstanding you mother, for testing you and for questioning your mothering. If not for you mom, I could never have understood myself. I thank you for your caring hands and your equally caring fists.

THE LAST VISIT FROM THE GIRL IN THE WILLOW TREE
First Place, Memoir, Annual Prison Writing Contest, PEN America
Zeke

She came at a complex time—we all knew it, she did too. She made the trip all the way from Boston, had bundled it with her summer plans to go back home in the suburb outside of Milwaukee she grew up in. She took a hammer and busted a chunk of her summer just to come see me when my life was on the line, behind glass in jailhouse oranges. It was still within that time when the very real fear of apocalypse was entangled with the lofty dreams that I could still go home—that I would go home—that I could reinvent my dreams, be that someone else, still young but wise and triumphant. That maybe I could be with her, that it should happen and that it all would—even though it was becoming clearer that I was going away, I just didn't know for how long.

Now she was here—the real person that drove with my mom over an hour from Minneapolis to the small jailhouse in the middle of the plainest town in Minnesota. I knew she was coming, but I could never be prepared. My hair and sparse beard that sprouts in odd patterns just couldn't be right enough. We had been writing letters during the whole process, I had a friend go and find her. I couldn't help but tell her about the Hennepin county jail with the green roof; old and rotten little corners that felt haunted. I told her about the nightmares I would have; waking up in sweats, realizing I was still there on a bunk, in a dorm that smelled like bologna and orange peels. It was a sober experience that humbled and reconstructed me. She sent me a picture of her in the red graduation gown and degree from the university she went to. It was the evidence of an obvious contrast in the directions the two of us had taken in our lives. It helped me craft a delusion that somehow even in my delinquency I could live vicariously through her light. The background had changed dramatically from when we used to drink whatever beer we could steal from our parents' refrigerators, and sit in a cabin throwing abstract teenage philosophy in the air and let it float with all the smoke in the air.

...

I started to realize a long time ago it was probably never fair to call this person the love of my life, especially after all that time passed, but maybe it's because it's so damn hard to see things as anything but the same as when I left it—like the views of the city I'd seen growing up, from random angles on top of abandoned buildings, from the windows of houses I only ever looked through once, or horizons from hilltops that made colors move like I never saw again. I can remember the images, even rustle up feelings associated with them, but I have no idea where any of them are now, or if they even still exist. And of all the teenage crushes that grow up and dissipate into the air, why should this one mean anything other than it did? Probably because I went away, and no one took that place. Life went on for everybody but stayed the same for all of us that got our feet stuck in the concrete of these institutions.

But I still think about her, even as others have come through my life—I always have. I would wonder where she was now—who she married—what she became—what her kids looked like. Did she still go to the cabin? How would she act if she saw me again as the person I was now after being where I was all these years? I was told once about someone we grew up with who went away for a long time when we were young, that "He's always gonna think the world and everyone in it is the same as when he left it." I wonder if that's how those out there feel about us. Maybe that's why so many people out there don't return letters or pick up the phone when I call. I wonder if some of those people would rather we just stay the same person, the same image as they remember, that way they can love or hate us, or stay as indifferent as they ever wanted to. At that last visit I remember her asking me if I remembered what her favorite tree was; I didn't, I was too preoccupied with my own world, my own persona to remember. I was ashamed, of all the things I could remember; names, dates, times, and contexts—but I couldn't remember something I'm sure she wholly intended for me to. Maybe if I had remembered she would have stuck around. Maybe if I hadn't turned down that certain street, or gone out that particular night—maybe if I hadn't quit that particular job, or maybe if I hadn't protected my pride so much or had been tougher, and less afraid—maybe if I had just been braver things would have been better. And even if I had, there would always be something else I should have done, the do-over that would never be done over. Things happen all the time, and I catalog them as things she might've laughed at- songs I wondered if she would like—if by now they probably just reminded her of other people or experiences. In the darkness, I had run up ahead hastily to see what was there and came back to where she was waiting just to tell her there was just more darkness.

Conclusion

It is true, as Patrick Berry (2018) points out, that it is easy to romanticize, even fetishize the writing of the incarcerated. It's easy to become too naive, too optimistic, even too patronizing about what literacy education might do for those who live behind bars. There needs to be some sort of balance between, on the one hand, pathologizing and recriminalizing the incarcerated and, on the other hand, overlooking the realities of their crimes and their victims in an attempt to make amends for the societal factors that contributed to their life arc and the unfortunate decisions they made along the way.

Sometimes, the writing of the incarcerated is presented in a decontextualized, precious way, like a form of outsider art. The purpose of the selections offered here is to provide evidence of the central argument of the book:

Behind bars live people who are intelligent, creative, and empathetic human beings, even in the face of the terrible actions that put them there. Liberal arts education can indeed transform the self-narratives of those human beings as well as their attitudes, perspectives, and future behavior. As Christopher Zoukis, himself an incarcerated writer, writes in *College for Convicts: The Case for Higher Education in American Prisons* (2014):

> Prisoner-students discover that their identity can be defined as something other than criminals. Each milestone achieved during classwork builds self-esteem. They can envision a life built on principles and techniques other than crime.
>
> Change—lasting change, meaningful change, the kind of change that transforms—comes from within. No other process or procedure is as capable of creating that kind of change except education.

If, as a society, we choose to keep alive those who commit serious crimes, then we need to keep them human. The humanities are well named. Through education, through reading, and through writing, the incarcerated can reclaim their humanity, learn empathy, and find creative and constructive ways of expressing and facing the pain that was a part of their journey to their crimes. They can also learn to acknowledge the pain their actions caused others and to articulate the redemption they seek. They do it through their words, words no bars can hold.

Stay Free

Monday was Robert's last class. A big bear of a man, whose gentle demeanor is at odds with his appearance (and probably his record), Robert is being released on Monday, November 24th. This is a rare occurrence, since so many of the guys in our class are serving life sentences. These days, in our state anyway, most life sentences are really life sentences.

Robert undoubtedly committed a less serious crime than most of his classmates. In order to know why Robert is getting released, I'd have to know what he was in for and I am adamant about not trying to find that out, for any of them.

Robert's imminent release is bittersweet. What has been perhaps the hardest aspect of this experience has been the deep despair we feel when we think of the men we work with, incarcerated before they were twenty, often for crimes they committed or were convicted of before they were eighteen. Some are serving multiple life sentences, consecutively, and have ridiculous-sounding release dates like 2099. Last week, after Jason asked me if I could request that he be in the next class I taught, for no apparent reason, he said, "I'm 99 plus 17. 17. That's how old I was when they sent me to the maximum security prison."

So we respond to Robert's news with a strange mixture of optimism and wistfulness. His release underscores the impossibility of the eventual release of others. Our understanding that they have committed very serious crimes does not ameliorate this wistfulness, even if one might think it should.

Of course, the other element that renders Robert's release bittersweet is the ominous threat of recidivism. Nationwide, the average rate of the incarcerated reoffending within three years of release is more than two-thirds. Education in general and higher education in particular has, in multiple studies and metaanalyses, been found to be the single most effective tool against recidivism. Yet despite these statistics, it is hard to fund higher education, and the program in our state has very little money.

Higher education programs for the incarcerated are a tough sell, but this might be the only thing that works.

During our class break, I ask Robert if he would mind if I announce that tonight is his last class as well as explain the reason why. Robert says it's fine. "I'm gonna miss you all. I mean it," he says.

Right before class ends, I make the announcement. The class applauds, some looking at Robert, others looking down. Robert stands, and bows.

The guard comes to the door to signal the end of class. As the men straggle out, Mike, a quiet guy who keeps to himself and doesn't say much either to us or his fellow classmates, walks over to Robert.

"Hey, man, I know I didn't get to know you very well, but I admired how you represented yourself in this class. I wish I'd gotten to know you better, and I wanna wish you the best of luck."

"Thanks," says Robert. They shake hands.

"I mean it, man. Go out there, represent, do your thing. But, mostly, for all of us, stay free, man. You gotta stay free."

Thoughts Beyond the Bars: The Dark and the Light

I T HAD NEVER HAPPENED BEFORE in the history of my state. During the writing of this book, a corrections officer was killed by a prisoner in the prison where I teach. Since then, everything has changed. As painful as it is, it would be dishonest not to include this horrific event in the exploration of teaching and learning behind bars that this book has attempted to provide.

In these pages, I have argued that the power of literacy and engagement with the liberal arts can help redirect the energies of the incarcerated and help rewrite their personal narratives. I have argued that the men with whom I work are, by and large, not bad people but good people who have done something bad. As Willie X, one of my formerly incarcerated students, says, "Everybody's better than the worst they've ever done." I have argued that the men, and our society as a whole, can benefit from offering the incarcerated the ability to pursue liberal arts education and that they both need and deserve, yes, deserve, the opportunity to express themselves through writing.

I have tried not to oversell the notion that literacy is a panacea that can ameliorate all the ills of the carceral state; I have tried not to overromanticize the enterprise of education behind bars; and I have tried not to valorize my own efforts or the efforts of the others who teach "behind the fence." I have tried not to be naive about who the men before me in my classroom are. Yet, at the same time, I give them credit for their resilience, for their intelligence, and most of all for their humanity. I operate from a place of hope and optimism, as do nearly all of the corrections personnel I have met.

This incident has shaken everyone in the prison to his core. The details of the attack are unclear. A single prisoner attacked a guard in an industrial wing with a hammer and two homemade knifes. No one else was involved, and other guards came too late to help. The motivation is even more unclear than the details of the attack. The entire prison system, including all correctional facilities within the state, was immediately put on lockdown. All educational events, including ongoing classes, were canceled. All volunteers were refused entry. All sympathy for the incarcerated seemed to evaporate statewide as people came to grips with the tragedy. The attacker was sent to another prison facility and is awaiting trial. He was already serving a long sentence for murder, although he was within five years of his out date.

Several corrections officers immediately quit in the aftermath of the attack, citing unheeded warnings of understaffing and increasingly dangerous conditions. Other employees found themselves weak-kneed as they entered the place of employment. Counselors were brought in; the commissioner of Corrections could not contain his tears during a press conference about the incident. The people with whom I work in education spoke to me shakily on the phone. "We can't cope with this," one told me.

In the meantime, all of the prisoners were confined indefinitely to their cells, without pens, pencils, paper, paint, or any hope for future educational opportunities. The local project of rehabilitation—through classes, workshops, meetings, services—came to a screeching halt. Things will eventually return to whatever "normal" is in a prison. But I am haunted by this grim reminder that the prison isn't just like any other place filled with ordinary people. As the beloved education director told me in our first conversation after the incident, "Well, this is a reminder of where we work, Deborah." The incident occurred in the last week of her twenty-year career. Her retirement celebration, which was to include a presentation of a volume of more than one hundred letters of gratitude from prisoners with whom she had worked, was canceled. "What a way to end," she said somberly. "I just need to remember the good."

So, does this mean that our efforts to decriminalize and humanize the men with whom we work are in vain?

We are all mourning. Not just for a valiant life that was lost, but for the opportunity to think with generosity and without fear of the incarcerated. Yes, one single person committed this murder. But much more than an individual guard was murdered that day in the industrial wing of my prison.

The Light: Eli on the Other Side of the School-to-Prison Pipeline

The murder of the guard was a grim reminder of the brutal realities of the carceral state and the complexity of the population of those who live behind bars. It is a cautionary tale, one that prevents me or any other well-intentioned but often naive teachers from drawing a rosy and unrealistic portrait of literacy endeavors behind bars. At the same time, it is critical not to let the indefensible actions and their consequences of one prisoner color our perception of the incarcerated and become a defining image.

At 7:30 a.m. on a still, cold March morning, I wait inside the entrance of an urban public high school with Patrick, a ninth-grade English teacher, on one side of me and a security guard on the other. We are waiting for the arrival of Eli, my formerly incarcerated student, who has agreed to spend the day at the high school. Eli arrives exactly at 7:30, dressed immaculately in a three-piece gray suit. I berate myself silently for worrying that he might be late.

Together, Eli, Patrick, and I make our way through the crowded halls; nearly every student we see is a student of color. The ninth-grade students have been reading Walter Mosley's *Always Outnumbered, Always Outgunned*, an adolescent novel about the challenges of adjustment faced by an African American ex-convict. Patrick, an extraordinarily gifted veteran teacher committed to the urban youth he serves, has become increasing worried about the precarious pathway of many of his students. They seem to be gingerly walking the tightrope between jail and college. Many have experienced the ravages of incarceration in their own families—fathers, brothers, uncles, even sisters and mothers. Patrick hopes to interest them in learning in ways that so many of my incarcerated students were not. He wants to engage them in literacy, in reading texts and writing about them. He also wants his literacy lessons to be relevant.

During my regular visits to Patrick's classroom, he and I hatched a plan, inspired in part by a student named Henry. Henry is bright and thoughtful, but he is flunking out of ninth grade. He is frequently absent, tardy to class when he is present, his sweatshirt hood hiding his face. He never participates in class. Patrick is worried about Henry, and so am I. He seems destined to drop out of school. The enticements of the streets beckon. If only we could fashion learning to capture Henry before the police do.

Patrick decides to teach the Walter Mosley book and asks if I'd like to come speak to his classes about my experiences teaching in the prison. Mindful of Erica Meiner's (2007) insightful conceptualization of the White Lady Bountiful, I tell Patrick that my speaking to his students might be no more effective than Nancy Reagan's "Just Say No" campaign in the 1980s. I am not a messenger with any credibility.

But Eli is. Incarcerated at age fifteen for more than nineteen years before managing to have his life sentence overturned, Eli knows the consequences of poor choices only too well. In addition to describing the realities of prison, with which the students are almost morbidly fascinated, he also speaks passionately about the power of education. He falls into the cadence of a preacher and uses a call-and-response to rouse the ninth graders.

"Hey y'all, I wouldn't be here without education. Say 'education.'"

The students respond, "Education."

"I needed to release the power of my own intellect. Say 'intellect.'"

"Intellect."

"I needed to learn that literacy is the key. It was the key to my freedom. Say 'freedom.'" "Freedom." Henry looks up.

"Brother, I am speaking to you. Do you hear me?"

Henry nods slowly.

"I am out here to make sure you don't go in. It's what I am dedicating my life to. Hear me, little brother, stay free. Stay in school. Say I will, say I will, y'all."

"I will." Henry mouths the words.

High school student listening to Eli

Eli teaching high school

Eli, Patrick, and I all know that it will take more than a one-time visit by a formerly incarcerated person to keep Henry out of prison. But as much as this story is about Henry, it's about Eli, too. I flash back to that meeting at the restaurant that opened this book and remember Eli's vow to turn his attention to the social conditions that caused him to land in prison. Eli has recrafted himself from a discarded shell of a man known only by an ID number, written off by everyone except himself, to a vibrant example of the power of literacy behind bars.

Yes, prisons are inhabited by those who have not learned any path besides violence, people like the man who attacked the prison guard, but they are also filled with men like Eli, who will embrace and return the lessons of literacy, if we are willing to offer them.

REFERENCES

Alexander, M. (2010). *The new Jim Crow: Mass incarceration in the age of colorblindness*. New York/London: The New Press.

Appleman, D. (1999). *Critical encounters in high school English: Teaching literary theory to adolescents*, 1st edition. New York: Teachers College Press.

Appleman, D. (2009). *Critical encounters in high school English: Teaching literary theory to adolescents*, 2nd edition. New York: Teachers College Press.

Appleman, D. (2013). Teaching in the dark: The promise and pedagogy of creative writing in prison. *English Journal*, 102:4.

Appleman, D. (2014). *Radicalizing the literature methods class through critical literary theory in reclaiming English language arts methods courses: Critical issues and challenges for teacher educators in top-down times*. Webb, A., and Brass, J., eds. New York: Routledge.

Appleman, D. (2016). Word by word: Teaching poetic economy behind bars. In *Fostering literacy behind bars: Successful strategies and services for incarcerated youth and adults*. Albright, K., Gavigan, K., and Styslinger, M., eds. Lanham, MD: Rowman and Littlefield Publishers.

Aizer, A., and Doyle, J. (July 16, 2013). What is the long term impact of incarcerating juveniles? *Vox CEPR Policy Portal*. Retrieved from https://voxeu.org/article/what-long-term-impact-incarcerating -juveniles.

Baca, J. S. (2001). *A place to stand*. New York: Grove Press.

Baca, J. S. (2009). Preface. In *From the inside out: Letters to young men and other writings*. New York: Student Press Initiative, p. 13.

Bahena, S., Cooc, N., Currie-Rubin, R., Kuttner, P., and Ng, M., eds. (2012). *Disrupting the school-to-prison pipeline*. Cambridge, MA: Harvard Educational Review.

Bard College. (n.d.). Bard Prison Initiative. Retrieved from http://www.bpi.bard.edu.

Bates, L. (2013). *Shakespeare saved my life: Ten years in solitary with the bard*. Naperville, IL: Sourcebooks.

Berry, P. (2018). *Doing time, writing lives: Refiguring literacy and higher education in prison*. Carbondale: Southern Illinois University Press.

Betts, R.D. (2009). *A question of freedom: A memoir of learning, survival, and coming of age in prison*. New York: Penguin.

Brown University (2013). *Liberal learning goals*. Retrieved from http://brown.edu/Administration/Dean_of_the_College/curriculum/downloads/Lib_Learning_Goals.pdf.

Buber, M. (1958). *I and thou*, 2nd edition. R.G. Smith, trans. New York: Charles Scribner's Sons.

Casella, R. (2003). Punishing dangerousness through preventive detention: Illustrating the institutional link between school and prison. *New Directions for Youth Development*, 2003(99): 55–70.

Christensen, L. (2017). *Reading, writing and rising up: Teaching about social justice and the power of the written word*, 2nd edition. Milwaukee, WI: Rethinking Schools Ltd.

Davis, S. W. (2011). Inside-out: The reaches and limits of a prison program. In *Razor wire women: Prisoners, activists, scholars and artists*. Lawston, J. M., and Lucas, A. E., eds. Albany: State University of New York Press; pp. 203–23.

Dewey, J. (1916). *Democracy and education: An introduction to the philosophy of education*. New York: Macmillan.

DuVernay, A., Barish, H., and Averick, S. (Producers), & DuVernay, A. (Director). (2016). *13th* [Motion Picture]. United States: Kandoo Films.

Franklin, H. B. (2008). Can the penitentiary teach the academy to read? *PMLA*, 123(3): 643–48.

Greenberg, E., Dunleavy, E., and Kutner, M. (2007). Literacy behind bars: Results from the 2003 national assessment of adult literacy prison survey. U.S. Department of Education, NCES 2007-473.

Grinnell College. Liberal arts in prison. Retrieved from http://www.grinnell.edu/academic/prisonprogram.

Harris, R. (March 14, 1991). On the purpose of a liberal arts education. Retrieved from http://www.virtualsalt.com/libarted.htm.

hooks, b. (1994). *Outlaw culture: Resisting representations.* New York: Routledge.

Karpowitz, D. (2017). *College in prison: Reading in an age of mass incarceration.* New Brunswick, NJ: Rutgers University Press.

Kim, C. Y., Losen, D. J., and Hewitt, D. T. (2010). *The school-to-prison pipeline: Structuring legal reform.* New York: New York University Press.

King, M. L. (February 1947). The purpose of education. *Maroon Tiger* (10). Retrieved from https://kinginstitute.stanford.edu/king-papers/documents/purpose-education.

Kohl, H. (1991). *I won't learn from you!: The role of assent in learning.* Minneapolis: Milkweed Editions.

Kunen, J. S. (2017). Opening minds behind bars. *Columbia Magazine,* 21–27.

Lave, J., and Wenger, E. (1991). *Situated learning: Legitimate peripheral participation (Learning in doing: Social, cognitive and computational perspectives),* 1st edition. Cambridge, UK: Cambridge University Press.

Lee, S. J. (2001). More than "model minorities" or "delinquents": A look at Hmong American high school students. *Harvard Educational Review,* 71(3): 505–28.

Lewen, J. (2008). Academics belong in prison: On creating a university at San Quentin. *PMLA,* 123(3): 688–96.

Lonetree, A. (May 12, 2018). At St. Paul's Johnson High School, students "do more for themselves." *Star Tribune.* Retrieved from http://www.startribune.com/at-st-paul-s-johnson-high-students-do-more-for-themselves/482462421/.

Mader, J., and Butrymowicz, S. (2014). Pipeline to prison: Special education too often leads to jail for thousands of American children. *The Hechinger Report.* Retrieved from https://hechingerreport.org/pipeline-prison-special-education-often-leads-jail-thousands-american-children/.

Manthripragada, A. (2018). Freedom within limits: The penc(cil) is mightier. In Lockard, J., and Rankins-Robertson, S., eds., *Prison pedagogies: Learning and teaching with imprisoned writers*. Syracuse, NY: Syracuse University Press, pp. 50–87.

Martin, M. (June 2, 2009). What happened to prison education programs? Retrieved from https://socialistworker.org/2009/06/02/what-happened-to-prison-education.

Maslow, A. H. (1943). A theory of human motivation. *Psychological Review*, 50(4): 370–96.

Meiners, E. R. (2007). *Right to be hostile: Schools, prisons, and the making of public enemies*. New York: Routledge.

Meiners, E. R. (2016). *For the children?: Protecting innocence in a carceral state*. Minneapolis: University of Minnesota Press.

Minnesota Department of Corrections (August 8, 2018). *Minnesota correctional facility—Stillwater inmate profile*. Retrieved from https://coms.doc.state.mn.us/tourreport/01FacilityInmateProfile.pdf.

National Association for the Advancement of Colored People Legal Defense Fund. (2005). *Dismantling the school-to-prison-pipeline*. Retrieved from http://www.naacpldf.org/publication/dismantling-school-prison-pipeline.

National Commission on Writing in America's Schools and Colleges. (2003). *The neglected "R": The need for a writing revolution*. Retrieved from https://www.nwp.org/cs/public/download/nwp_file/21478/the-neglected-r-college-board-nwp-report.pdf?x-r=pcfile d.

Nixon, V. (December 18, 2012). During and after incarceration, education changes lives. *New York Times*. Retrieved from http://www.nytimes.com/roomfordebate/2012/12/18/prison-could-be-productive/during-and-after-incarceration-education-changes-lives.

Noguera, P. (Autumn 2003). Schools, prisons, and social implications of punishment: Rethinking disciplinary practices. *Theory Into Practice*, 42(4), *Classroom Management in a Diverse Society*, pp. 341–50.

Nolan, K. (2011). *Police in the hallways: Discipline in an urban high school*. Minneapolis: University of Minnesota Press.

Oates, J. C., ed. (2014). *Prison noir*. New York: Akashic Books.

Palmer, P. (1999). *The courage to teach: Exploring the inner landscape of the teacher's life*. Hoboken, NJ: John Wiley and Sons, Inc.

Paul, M. (1991). *When words are bars: a guide to literacy programming in correctional institutions.* Kitchener, Ontario: Core Literacy.

Pew Center on the States. (February 28, 2009). One in 100: Behind bars in America 2008. Retrieved from http://www.pewtrusts.org/our_work_report_detail.aspx?id=35900.

Prose, F. (2006). *Reading like a writer: A guide for people who love books and want to write them.* New York: HarperCollins.

Rogers, L. (Spring 2008). Finding our way from within: Critical pedagogy in a prison writing class. *Open Words*, 2(1).

Rose, M. (February 28, 2013). What teachers can do for returning adult students. Blog post. Retrieved from https://evolllution.com/opinions/what-teachers-can-do-for-returning-adult-students/.

Salzman, M. (2004). *True notebooks: A writer's year at juvenile hall.* New York: Vintage Books.

Schworm, P. (2008). In digital era, blue books still causing white knuckles. Retrieved from http://archive.boston.com/news/local/articles/2008/10/24/in_digital_era_blue_books_still_causing_white_knuckles/.

Shailor, J. (2008). When muddy flowers bloom: The Shakespeare Project at Racine Correctional Institution. *PMLA*, 123(3): 632–41.

Sieben, L. (May 5, 2011). Report describes limits of inmates' access to college education. *Chronicle of Higher Education.* Retrieved from https://www.chronicle.com/article/Inmates-Access-to-College/127375.

Smith, M. W., and Wilhem, J. D. (2002). *"Reading don't fix no chevies": Literacy in the lives of young men.* Portsmouth, NH: Heinneman.

Stevenson, B. (2015). *Just mercy: The story of justice and redemption.* New York: Spiegel and Grau.

Tatum, A. (2005). *Teaching reading to black adolescent males: Closing the achievement gap.* Portsmouth, NH: Stenhouse Publishers.

Tatum, A. (2009). *Reading for their life: (Re)building the textual lineages of African American adolescent males.* Portsmouth, NH: Heinneman.

Teske, S. C., and Huff, J. B. (2011). When did making adults mad become a crime?: The court's role in dismantling the school-to-prison pipeline. *Juvenile and Family Justice Today*, winter: 14–17.

Trounstine, J. R. (2008). Beyond prison education. *PMLA*, 123(3): 674–77.

Vaught, S. E. (2017). *Compulsory: Education and the dispossession of youth in a prison school.* Minneapolis: University of Minnesota Press.

Wagner, P. (August 28, 2012). Incarceration is not an equal opportunity punishment. Retrieved from https://www.prisonpolicy.org/articles/notequal.html.

Waxler, R. P. (2008). Changing lives through literature. *PMLA*, 123(3): 678–83.

Wenger, E. (1999). *Communities of practice: Learning, meaning, and identity (Learning in doing: Social, cognitive and computational perspectives)*, 1st edition. Cambridge, UK: Cambridge University Press.

Winn, M. (2018). *Justice on both sides: Transforming education through restorative justice.* Cambridge, MA: Harvard Educational Press.

Xiong, S. Y. (2012). Hmong Americans' educational attainment: Recent changes and remaining challenges. *Hmong Studies Journal*, 13(2): 1–18.

Yagelski, R. P. (2000). *Literacy matters: Writing and reading the social self.* New York: Teachers College Press.

Zoukis, C. (2014). *College for convicts: The case for higher education in American prisons.* Jefferson, NC: McFarland & Company.

Zuber, T., and Berg-Jacobson, A. (March 14, 2017). Diversifying the teacher workforce through Grow Your Own: A snapshot of three programs. Blog post. Retrieved from http://blog.apastyle.org/apastyle/2016/04/how-to-cite-a-blog-post-in-apa-style.html.

SELECTIONS OF WRITING BY INCARCERATED WRITERS

"A Certain Kind," 63–65
"A Day at the Zoo," 131–32
"Black Lives Don't Matter," 75–78
"Jasmine," 79–81
"My Mother and My Mom," 133–37
"People I Know," 86–90
"Prison Is," 127–28
"Prison Pastoral," 126–27
"Red Wagon," 128–29
"Relinquished Notes," 127
"Several Questions," 71–72
"Smurphs on the Wall," 62
"That Picture on the Wall," 65–67
"The Last Visit from the Girl in the Willow Tree," 135–137
"The Mother's Lament," 124–26
"These Songs Remind Me," 83–86
"U Wouldn't Understand," 129–30
"What I Have Been Doing," 72
"Where I Am From," 122
"Where I Am From," 123–24
"Where I'm From," 121–22

INDEX

Advanced Creative Writing class
    "public" readings in, 41
Aizer, A., 107
Alexander, M., 2, 22, 59, 105, 111
alternate identity
    ability to craft, 46–47
alternative narratives
    liberal arts education and, 46–47
Always Outnumbered, Always Out-
    gunned, 110–11, 143
A Passage to India
    colonialism in, 24
attention
    individual, 38

Baca, J.S., 31, 44 45, 47, 60, 83
Baldwin, J., 25, 99, 113
"ban the box" movement, 22
Bard College
    "liberal arts behind bars" from, 3
Bard Prison Initiative, 23
behavioral changes
    writing programs and, 5
Berry, P., 42, 43, 120, 137
Black Lives Matter movement, 75
blog entries
    "Fist Bump Through the Bars,"
        9–10
    "How to Do a Full Body Workout
        in Your Cell," 17–18, 18*f*

"Knowledge Is Truly Food For Our
    Souls," 56–56
"Lesson Planning in Prison," 17–18,
    18*f*
"Saying Goodbye to Grandma in
    Chains," 40
"School-to-Prison Pipeline," 116–17
"Stay Free," 139–40
"Sticks and Stones" essay, 94–97
"Tony and the Blue Book," 28–30
Boys of Hope Program, 112
Brown University
    on results of liberal arts education,
        3–4
Buber, M., 34, 36
Bureau of Justice
    Prison Policy Initiative of, 81

Chan, C., 96
Chan, J., 96
Christensen, L., 121
class(es)
    prisoners learning about, 14
classroom(s)
    prison *see* prison classroom
Coates, T-N, 25
collective
    writers', 49–50
college education
    prison education *vs.,* 25–26

College for Convicts: The Case for Higher Education in American Prisons, 138
College in Prison, 14
colonialism
  in *A Passage to India*, 24
communication
  teacher–student, 38
communities of practice (CoP)
  criteria for, 48
  described, 48–49
  situated, 48–50
conference(s)
  prohibited by prisons, 38
connection
  between heart of teacher and heart of student, 35
constraint(s)
  on teacher–student relationship, 34
control
  of inmates, 31–40
CoP. *see* communities of practice (CoP)
correctional facilities. *see also* prison(s)
  Shakespeare productions by and for offenders at, 5
court involvement and detention
  in school-to-prison pipeline, 107
creative nonfiction
  by incarcerated writers, 132–37
creative writing
  emphasis on identity construction and narration in, 5, 6
  lack of, 103–4
  self-reflection in, 6
criminalization
  humanization *vs.*, 15

Dangerous Minds, 100
dehumanization
  incarceration and, 15, 58

Department of Corrections (DOC)
  training sessions by volunteers for, 37
Department of Corrections (DOC) personnel
  attending "public" readings, 41
detention
  in school-to-prison pipeline, 107
Dewey, J., 15, 20
dialogue
  essential to authentic learning, 34–35
disciplinary policies
  of schools, 101–2
"Dismantling the School to Prison Pipeline"
  of NAACP Legal Defense and Education Fund, 101–2
DOC. *see* Department of Corrections (DOC)
Doyle, J., 107
Duncan, E., 108

early court involvement and detention
  in school-to-prison pipeline, 107
educare
  defined, xvi
education
  in being rational, 26–27
  as central focus of incarceration, 82
  as cherished experience among incarcerated, 4
  as end unto itself, 4
  goals of, 39
  higher *see* higher education
  incarceration and, 1–10
  liberal, xv–xvi
  liberal arts *see* liberal arts education
  life or death, xv–xvi
  prison *vs.* college, 25–26
  purpose of, 20–21

recidivism effects of, 2, 6
self-expression and, 104
tension between incarceration and, 20
two-fold function of, 20
value of, xv–xvi
education programs in prison, 37
limitations on teacher–student interactions in, 38
restrictions on funding for, 2
engagement
with learning, 103
mutual, 48
enterprise
joint, 48

feminism
in *Pride and Prejudice*, 24
"Fist Bump Through the Bars," 9–10
flag
described, 11–12
Freedom Writers, 100
free verse
by incarcerated writers, 124–43
"free will"
loss of, 33
Freire, P., ix, 19, 24
From the Inside Out: Letters to Young Men and Other Writings, 5, 113
Frost, R., 24–25

GED courses
in prison, 47
geography of incarceration, 11–18
grief
writing as way to work through, 91
Grinnell College
"liberal arts behind bars" from, 3
Liberal Arts in Prison Program of, 4

Grow Your Own teacher-recruitment programs, 107–8

haiku
by incarcerated writers, 120–21
hallways
policing school, 106–7
Harris, R., 3
higher education
appropriateness within prisons, 5
for the incarcerated, 1–10
high schools. *see also* school(s)
lack of writing in, 103–4
policing hallways in, 106–7
role in path to incarceration, 100–17
zero-tolerance policies of, 105–6
Hmong
described, 69
incarcerated, 69
"hole," 26, 33
"How to Do a Full Body Workout in Your Cell," 17–18, 18f
Hughes, L., 74, 118–19
humanization
criminalization vs., 15

identity(ies)
alternate, 46–47
literacy and, 42
identity construction
in creative writing, 5, 6
"identity" research
focus of, 42
incarcerated
creative writing for, 5
education as cherished experience among, 4
higher education for, 1–10
as invisible, 2
liberal arts education for, 1–10

incarcerated (*continued*)
  literacy as transformative power
    for, 43–46
  literacy learning of, 5
  literature's impact on lives of, 5
incarcerated learners
  profiles of, 58–97, 68*f*
incarcerated writers
  intelligence, aptitude, and talent
    among, 92
  mental health issues among,
    92–93
  samples from, 58–97, 68*f*
  selections from, 120–37 *see also*
    specific writings and writing
    selections
  as "the cream of the crop," 92
  writing selections by, 120–37 *see*
    also specific writings and writing
    selections
incarceration
  dehumanization in, 15, 58
  education as central focus of, 1–10,
    82
  geography of, 11–18
  goals of, 39
  of Hmong, 69
  of juveniles, 107
  lack of interest in school prior to,
    93
  literacy effects on, 47–48
  mass, 22, 58
  path to, 100–17
  poverty and, 59
  prevalence of, 2
  race in, 59, 81
  tension between education and, 20
  in US, 1–2
individual attention
  prohibited by prisons, 38

inmate(s)
  control of, 31–40
  surveillance of, 31–40
Institute for Higher Education Policy,
  2–3
Introduction to Literature course, 24,
  73, 99
"I Will Write Myself Out of Prison,"
  41–57
I Won't Learn From You, 36

James, J., 21
Jim Crow laws, 101
joint enterprise
  in CoP, 48
*Justice on Both Sides: Transforming
  Education Through Restorative
  Justice*, 108
"Just Say No" campaign, 144
juvenile(s)
  societal costs of incarcerating, 107
Juvenile and Family Justice Today, 106

Karpowitz, D., 14, 23, 25–26, 120
King, M.L., Jr., 20, 21, 27
"Knowledge Is Truly Food For Our
  Souls," 56–57
Kohl, H., 36

Lave, J., 48
learner(s)
  incarcerated *see* incarcerated
    learners
learning
  dialogue essential to, 34–35
  lack of engagement with, 103
  for learning's sake, xv, 120
  literacy, 5
  students' perceptions related to, 36
Lee, B., 97

legislation
  tough-on-crime, 2
"Lesson Planning in Prison," 17–18,
  18*f*
letter(s)
  to teachers, 38
"Letter to My Nephew," 113
"liberal arts behind bars"
  from Bard College and Grinnell
    College, 3
liberal arts education
  alternative narratives provided by,
    46–47
  Brown University on, 3–4
  described, 3
  expressing one's ideas and learning
    through writing in, 4–5
  focus of, 120
  for incarcerated, 1–10
  in teaching one how to think, 4
  value of, xv–xvi
Liberal Arts in Prison Program
  of Grinnell College, 4
library
  prison, 2, 13
life of the mind behind bars
  nature of, 21–22
literacy, 43
  identity and, 42
  incarceration impacted by, 47–48
  as possibility, 43
  through writing, 47
  as transformative power of incarcer-
    ated, 43–46
literacy learning
  of incarcerated, 5
literacy learning experiences
  benefits of, 6
literacy skills
  undeveloped, 103–4

literary pursuit in prison
  purity of, 78–79
literature
  impact on lives of incarcerated, 5
Lloyd, W.E., Jr., ix
Lolita
  misogyny in, 24
Lyons, G.E., 121, 122

Manthripragada, A., 13–15, 21
Martin, M., 2
Maslow, A., 81
mass incarceration, 58
  as New Jim Crow, 22
Meiners, E., 36, 43, 100–1, 144
memoirs
  by incarcerated writers, 132–37
  six-word, 121
mental health issues
  among prison writers, 92–93
misogyny
  in *Lolita*, 24
Morrison, T., 25
Mosley, W., 110–11, 143, 144
murder of prison guard, 141–46
mutual engagement
  in CoP, 48

NAACP Legal Defense and Educa-
    tion Fund
  "Dismantling the School to Prison
    Pipeline" of, 101–2
narration
  in creative writing, 5, 6
narrative(s)
  alternative, 46–47
New Jim Crow, 105
  mass incarceration as, 22
newspapers
  prison, 5, 21–22

New York Times Sunday Magazine, 25

Nin, A., 60

Nixon, V., 4

"No Hugs for Thugs," 31–40

Nolan, K., 106

nonfiction

creative, 132–37

Oates, J.C., 31, 83

Offender Identification Numbers (OIDs), 58

"offenders"

prisoners as, 37

OIDs. *see* Offender Identification Numbers (OIDs)

Palmer, P., 35, 36

Panopticon, 39

path to incarceration, 100

public schools' role in, 100–17

Pell Grants

restrictions on funding, 2–3

penal institutions

punishment in, 1

PEN Prison Writing contest

award winning poem, 86–90

PEN writing awards, 83

Perry, W., 24

phone calls

to teachers, 38

"pill run," 58

PMLA, 5

poem(s). *see also specific poem*

award winning, 86–90

where I'm from, 121–24

poet(s)

from illiterate to, 44–45

Police in the Hallways, 106

policing school hallways

in school-to-prison pipeline, 106–7

poverty

incarceration and, 59

practice

situated communities of, 48–50

Pride and Prejudice

feminism in, 24

prison(s). *see also* correctional facilities

appropriateness of higher education within, 5

becoming man in, 73

as departments of punishment, 11

divisions in, 24

dynamics of working in, 12

educational offerings in, 37

education programs in, 2

funding for education programs in, 2

GED courses in, 47

layout of, 11

literary pursuit in, 78–79

as misleading places, 11–18

nature of life of mind in, 21–22

people in *see* incarcerated

process of entering, 12–13

punishment in, 1

reading ideology of controlled environment of, 25

Shakespeare productions by and for offenders at, 5

prison classroom

divisions in, 24

goal of, 14

as sanctuary, 13

surveillance invading culture of, 32

prison education

college education *vs.*, 25–26

prisoner(s)

manipulating/taking advantage of volunteers, 37

as "offenders," 37

prison guard
    murder of, 141–46
prison library, 2, 13
prison newspapers
    content of, 21–22
    writing programs contributing to, 5
Prison Policy Initiative
    from Bureau of Justice, 81
prison writers. *see* writer(s)
Prison Writers' Collective, 111–12
Prose, F., 118
Proust, M., 60
"public" readings
    in Advanced Creative Writing class,
        41
    DOC personnel attending, 41
public schools. *see also* school(s)
    failing, 102
    lack of writing in, 103–4
    policing hallways in, 106–7
    role in path to incarceration, 100–17
    zero-tolerance policies of, 105–6
punishment
    penal institutions and, 1
    prisons as departments of, 11
purity
    of literary pursuit in prison, 78–79

race
    as factor in incarceration, 59, 81
Race to Incarcerate, 111
rational
    education in being, 26–27
reading
    "public" *see* "public" readings
    for reading's sake, 120
    using critical lenses while, 25
Reading, Writing, and Rising Up, 121
Reagan, N., 144
recidivism
    education impact on, 2, 6

relationship(s)
    teacher–student *see* teacher–student
        relationship
repertoire
    shared, 48
research
    "identity," 42
restorative justice practices
    involving students, teachers, and
        administrators, 108–11
Restorative Justice Program, 6
rewriting of self, 41–57
Right to Be Hostile, 36
Rogers, L., 5
Rose, M., 35–36
Ross, M., 47–48

"Saying Goodbye to Grandma in
    Chains," 40
school(s). *see also* high schools; public
    schools
    disciplinary policies of, 101–2
    high *see* high schools
    lack of interest in, 93
    lack of writing in, 103–4
    opportunities for self-expression in,
        103–4
    policing hallways in, 106–7
    public *see* public schools
    role in path to incarceration,
        100–17
    zero-tolerance policies of, 105–6
school hallways
    policing, 106–7
school-to-prison pipeline
    court involvement and detention in,
        107
    described, 101–2
    failing public schools as entry point
        to, 102
    interrupting, 98–117

school-to-prison pipeline (*continued*)
  lack of engagement with learning
    and, 103
  the other side of, 143–46, 145*f*
  policing school hallways in, 106–7
  zero-tolerance policies in, 105–6
"School-to-Prison Pipeline," 116–17
self
  rewriting of, 41–57
self-expression
  education and, 104
  little opportunity in schools for,
    103–4
self-reflection
  in creative writing, 6
Shakespeare productions
  by and for offenders at correctional
    facilities, 5
shared repertoire
  in CoP, 48
situated communities of practice
  (CoP), 48–50. *see also* communi-
    ties of practice (CoP)
six-word memoirs
  by incarcerated writers, 121
"Social Fathers," 112
societal costs
  of incarcerating juveniles, 107
"Song for the Genius Child," 118–19
"Songs from the Genius Child,"
  118–40
"Sonny's Blues," 99
Soto, G., 104–5
"Stay Free," 139–40
Stevenson, B., 15
"Sticks and Stones" essay, 94–97
student–teacher relationship. *see*
  teacher–student relationship
surveillance
  of inmates, 31–40

teacher(s)
  visitations by, 38
teacher-recruitment programs
  Grow Your Own, 107–8
teacher–student communication
  prohibited outside classroom, 38
teacher–student interactions
  limitations on, 38
teacher–student relationship
  centrality of, 36
  constraints placed on, 34
  importance of, 35–36
teaching
  as connection between teacher and
    students, 35
"telephone pole" layout, 11
testimony of transformation, 50–54
"the cream of the crop"
  writers as, 92
"the cure for any societal ills," 43
"the hole," 26, 33
The House I Live In, 111
the mind behind bars
  nature of life of, 21–22
The Neglected R, 103
The New Jim Crow, 111
"The Pie," 104–5
The Prison Mirror, 5, 21–22
"The Road Not Taken," 24–25
13th, 15, 111
Titus, B., 30
"Tony and the Blue Book," 28–30
tough-on-crime legislation, 2
transformation
  testimony of, 50–54

"Unlocking Potential: Results of a
  National Survey of Postsecondary Education in State Prisons,"
  2–3

visitation(s)
  by teachers, 38
volunteer(s)
  DOC, 37
  manipulating/taking advantage of, 37
  training sessions for, 37

Wenger, E., 48
"What If I Had Started to Write in High School?", 98–117
what we teach
  who we teach vs., xvi
where I'm from poems
  by incarcerated writers, 121–24
White Lady Bountiful (WLB), 43, 100, 144
who we teach
  what we teach vs., xvi
"Why Me?", 95
Williams, W.C., 124
Winn, M., 108–10
WLB. see White Lady Bountiful (WLB)
Wright, R., 25
writer(s)
  incarcerated see incarcerated writers

writers' collective, 49–50, 61–62
writer's statement(s)
  examples of, 50–54
writing
  creative see creative writing
  expressing one's ideas and learning through, 4–5
  literacy through, 47
  selections from incarcerated writers, 120–37 see also specific writings and writing selections
  as way to work through grief, 91
  for writing's sake, 120
"Writing in the Dark," 58–97, 68f
writing programs
  behavioral changes related to, 5
writing selections, 120–37
  creative nonfiction, 132–37
  free verse, 124–43
  haiku, 120–21
  memoirs, 121, 132–37
  six-word memoirs, 121
  where I'm from poems, 121–24

zero-tolerance policies
  in school-to-prison pipeline, 105–6
Zoukis, C., 138